Lois B. Hart, Ed.D.

Saying Hello:

Getting Your
Group Started

**Organization Design
and Development, Inc.**
King of Prussia, Pennsylvania
Publisher

Prepared for publication by Organization Design and Development, Inc. Printed in the United States of America.

First Printing: 1983
Second Printing: 1984
Second Edition: 1989

Library of Congress Catalog Card Number: 89-60051

ISBN: 0-925652-01-6

Contents

4   **Who Are We?**   91

Preface

From the beginning of my professional career over twenty years ago, I said "Hello" to many people: first to my young students in the sixth grade and later to adults who attended my workshops and speeches.

Quite truthfully, I did not pay much attention to how I introduced my presentations because I was more concerned about the body of my workshop or speech. However, my experience in Toastmasters forced me to pay closer attention to how I began my speeches. Suddenly I was aware of the critical importance of carefully planning what I said and did in the first few minutes of my workshops.

As I researched activities I could use, I discovered that there was no sourcebook of ideas. . .thus *Saying Hello: Getting Your Group Started* was born.

This collection consists of many new activities I have created and some old favorites rewritten to fit this new purpose.

Several of my professional colleagues have made contributions to this collection or have made suggestions for varying some of the existing activities. I am grateful to the following creative people: Dr. J. David Dalke, Rollin Glaser, Dr. Joel Goodman, Dr. John Jones, Vandla Julnes, Delores Leone, Margaret Rush, Dr. Marshall Sashkin, Dr. Sidney Simon, and Laurie Weiss.

All of these activities have been tested over and over with thousands of people. If you have an activity that consistently works for you or a creative variation on one found in this book, send it to the publisher for possible inclusion in a future edition of *Saying Hello*.

This book was originally published in 1983 through my company, Leadership Dynamics, and was reprinted three times. Rollin Glaser, President of Organization Design and Development, recognized its potential and offered to publish it in a new updated edition. We are proud of this new collection and know you will find it useful in your work.

There is a companion book called, *Saying Goodbye*. It also is a collection of creative activities that will help you end your group experience in a meaningful way.

Lois B. Hart, Ed.D.
Boulder, Colorado

January, 1989

Foreword

One of the most significant of the many contributions to the field of human resource development made by Bill Pfeiffer and John Jones was figuring out a way to share training activities with others in the field. Some of us still remember their first publication, a four inch by six inch spiral-bound "handbook" containing two dozen "structured experiences for human relations training," published in 1969 when their fledging consulting/publishing venture was headquartered in that urban center, Iowa City. Since then there have been many handbooks, from a variety of sources. Some have been great, a few not so great, and almost all have contained at least some useful "exercises" for use in training and HRD.

There remains a problem, however, despite the apparent abundance of training resources. Few of the many resources now available — thanks to John's and Bill's innovation — focus on a single topic or theme; most are compilations of activities cutting across a wide range of topics. When we saw the first edition of Lois Hart's *Saying Hello*, we knew immediately that here was a training resource that really filled an unmet need.

One of the most uncertain and potentially threatening times for a trainer, consultant, or HRD practitioner is that critical moment when one begins an event with a "new" group. Not even the most experienced or most blasé among us has not felt that instant of panic when it was time to "walk on stage." Not even the most skillful trainer we know has not wished for a bit more start-up time or a better start-up activity. That is what makes us sure that any active trainer will want Lois' structured experiences as a resource.

Lois did not just pull together some miscellaneous start-up exercises. She began by looking for the best, adapting them based on her own extensive experience as a trainer and HRD practitioner, and then sorting them into even more specific categories. *Saying Hello* is a distillation and refinement of the best that could be found.

As if that were not good enough, we asked Lois to revise her book, taking into account her experiences since it was first published. Finally, we each agreed to contribute a few "new" structured experiences — ones we had used and found to be especially effective.

This new revised edition of *Saying Hello* contains 66 structured exercises. Most experienced trainers will be familiar with at least a few of these, but we feel certain that no one will have seen most of them. Lois has retained her original classification scheme, which enables users to "fine tune" their designs and focus on or deal with some specific issue or problem in a particular group's start-up. We have enjoyed helping produce this revision and adding our own ideas. We are convinced that you will agree this is one of the more useful training resources in your library.

Marshall Sashkin
Rollin Glaser
John Jones

Introduction

People form their first impressions within one minute of meeting someone new or entering a new learning experience. Therefore, as trainers, facilitators, and group leaders we cannot afford to "get off on the wrong foot!" We need to plan carefully how we will introduce our workshops, meetings, and conferences so that participants will want to stay and hear more, so they will be receptive to meeting others, and so they will leave feeling that their time was well spent.

Saying Hello: Getting Your Group Started was written for planners of educational and training programs, meetings, and conferences. All of these experiences have to get started in some way, therefore, you might as well do it creatively and meaningfully.

You will notice that the word "facilitator" is used throughout the book to represent the various roles of group leader, trainer, educator, meeting leader, teacher, instructor, or seminar leader.

There are six chapters in this book. Here is a brief description of each one:

I. Introducing the Facilitator

These activities serve the purpose of introducing the facilitator, trainer, or group leader to the participants.

II. Clarifying Expectations and Objectives

These activities help participants to clarify their expectations and feelings, to identify their specific needs plus any resources they bring to this group experience.

Also the facilitator can clarify her/his own expectations, present the objectives and design of the program, and outline any ground rules.

III.
Who Are You?

These activities reveal information about the participants' uniqueness, values, ideas, interests, and experiences that will help increase their level of involvement in the group experience.

IV.
Who Are We?

These activities help the participants learn each others' names and identify what they have in common with one another. Many of the activities help to develop a sense of group teamwork and unity.

V.
Dipping into the Content

These activities help the participants get into the program's content while at the same time they are becoming better acquainted.

VI.
Regrouping Participants

These activities are used to re-group the participants at the same time they are getting better acquainted or because you have a need to form subgroups.

Here are the recommended steps to follow for selecting the most appropriate activity for your workshop or conference.

1. Identify the goal and objectives for your entire program. Once you have these stated, you can more easily select the best activities from this book.

    For example, if you have a one-day workshop, you might want to select an activity from Chapter V to immerse the participants into the program content during the warm-up segment. Or, if your program runs several days, you probably should select activities from Chapters I, II, and III to lay the foundation for the total experience. In addition, you might select a new activity from other chapters to use at the beginning of the morning and afternoon sessions.

2. Determine what you know about your participants. How many people will be attending? Did they know each other prior to this gathering? How do they feel about each other? How comfortable will they be disclosing personal information?

3. Determine how much time you can allot for one of these warm-up activities. Too often we skimp on this important part of our design, or even worse, skip it entirely!

   Each activity in this book indicates the approximate time required. Once you have selected an activity, leave enough time in your design for participants to complete the activity you have selected.

4. The matrix that follows this introduction is a handy reference for comparing the activities relative to their primary purpose, how many participants can be involved, and how much time is needed.

   For example, if you need an activity that will re-group your fifty participants but you only have fifteen minutes in your design, look down the appropriate columns listing these variables until you find the most appropriate activity.

5. Keeping your goal, program design, and participants in mind, review the activities from the most appropriate chapter.

   Each activity lists its objective(s), optimal group size, time needed, room set-up, supplies and equipment requirements, step-by-step instructions for facilitating the activity, and any variations you could try.

   Remember, a given activity might not fit your needs exactly so adapt, modify, mix, and match the activities.

6. After you use an activity, be sure to make notes on what you actually did, how it worked, and ideas for improvements for future use.

   You could enhance this book by adding other activities you have used in the past. Label them with the appropriate chapter, add them to your Table of Contents, and create an additional matrix for future reference.

Activity	Chapter						Group Size						Time				
	1	2	3	4	5	6	10	20	30	40	50	Any	15	30	45	60	+
Introducing the Facilitator																	
Hello! My Name Is. . .	●											●	●	●			
The Interview	●											●	●				
Let Me Introduce You To. . .	●											●	●				
Ask Me	●											●	●				
Clarifying Expectations and Objectives																	
Welcome to the Workshop		●										●	●	●			
Objectives and Guidelines		●										●	●				
Why Are You Here?		●										●		●			
The Whip		●							●				●	●			
The Magic Present		●							●					●			
Where Would You Rather Be?		●										●	●	●			
Folding Arms		●										●	●				
Issues and Obstacles		●										●		●	●		
Who Are You?																	
You Ought to Be in Pictures!			●				●	●	●	●	●			●			
The Exhibit Hall			●					●	●	●	●			●	●	●	
Resume		●	●									●		●			
The Name Tag			●									●		●	●	●	
The People Hunt			●		●			●	●	●	●			●	●		
What's in Your Wallet or Purse?			●					●					●				
Where Are You From?			●						●				●				
My Personal Shield			●									●		●			
Here's My Card			●									●		●	●	●	
What's in a Name			●									●	●				
Name Your Uniqueness			●						●				●				
First Impressions			●						●							●	
Post It			●						●				●	●			
The Picket Line			●									●		●			
I See Me As. . .			●									●		●			
Are You More. . .			●					●	●	●	●		●	●			
The Real Me			●									●		●			
You Can't Tell a Book. . .			●		●							●		●			
The Movie Screen			●									●		●			
Feelings Wheel			●									●	●	●			
Meet My Orange			●						●					●			

Activity	Chapter						Group Size						Time				
	1	2	3	4	5	6	10	20	30	40	50	Any	15	30	45	60	+
Who Are We?																	
Twenty Questions				●								●	●				
Around the Circle				●				●						●			
Name-Go				●			●	●	●					●			
How Many Hats Do We Wear?				●				●					●				
What's Your Sign?				●		●					●		●	●			
I'd Like You to Meet				●		●						●		●			
Tell Me More!				●								●		●			
Self-Sort				●								●		●			
Team Symbol				●								●				●	
The Builders				●								●		●	●	●	
The Trust Walk				●	●							●		●	●	●	
The Tie-Up				●								●		●	●	●	●
Sinking Ship				●						●						●	
The Machine				●			●	●						●			
Patterns				●	●			●	●	●	●			●	●		
Dipping into the Content																	
The Pre-Test						●						●	●	●	●	●	●
I Know. . . I Don't Know. . .						●			●					●	●	●	
Best/Worst						●					●		●	●			
The Computer						●	●						●				
Four Corners						●						●	●	●			
My Experience As. . .						●						●		●			
The Continuum						●			●				●	●			
Getting to Know You						●						●	●	●			
Re-grouping Participants																	
Colors or Numbers						●						●	●				
The Diversity Mix						●						●	●	●			
Meet and Match						●				●	●	●	●	●	●		
Mix and Mingle		●				●						●	●				
Team Signal						●						●	●				
I'm OK — You're OK						●						●	●				
The Five-Course Meal						●						●	●			●	●
Potpourri						●						●	●				
People to People						●						●	●				
All My Friends						●		●					●				

1

Introducing
the Facilitator

The activities in this first chapter serve the purpose of introducing the facilitator, trainer, or group leader to the participants.

Some are done very informally and yet set the stage for participants to interact with the facilitator. In addition, one activity shows the sponsor of the program how to introduce the facilitator to the participants.

Hello! My Name Is. . .

Objectives	To have the facilitator meet each participant personally and reduce any tendency to "elevate him/her to a pedestal"
	To learn something about each person that can be used during the workshop
Group Size	Works best with smaller groups, under twenty; with larger groups, only a sample will be greeted
Time Required	Approximately one minute per person
Physical Setting	Any setting
Materials Utilized	Name tags
Content and Process	1. While participants are checking in or waiting for the workshop to begin, the facilitator extends his/her hand and firmly shakes the participant's hand. Be sure to look the person in the eye and smile. Give your name as you want to be called. Repeat each person's name and make a personal comment based on what is on his/her name tag, such as where he/she is from or place of work.
	2. You could do your greeting in small groups where they are sitting or standing, but each person should be greeted personally.

Notes to Myself

The Interview

Objectives	To have participants learn something about the facilitator
	To model the behavior of disclosure to the participants
Group Size	Any size
Time Required	Ten minutes
Physical Setting	Any setting that allows the facilitator and interviewer to face the participants
Materials Utilized	For group size over forty, use a hand-mike

Content and Process

1. Prior to the workshop, discuss this idea with your sponsor or host. Explain that this method saves them the trouble of memorizing facts about you and gives the participants a chance to see the facilitator model behaviors that will be expected of them during the workshop.

2. When the sponsor starts the workshop, he/she explains to the participants that a new way of introducing the workshop facilitator will be used.

3. Select one participant to "interview" you. Indicate the questions you want asked of you. They might include three basic ones:
   > "What's your name?"
   > "Where are you from?"
   > "What do you do?"

4. Ask your interviewer to decide upon three more questions but not to tell you in advance. They should be questions that other participants might be thinking or would ask if they could. Examples might be:

    "What are you feeling right now?"
    "What is your career plan?"
    "What is your most effective time-saving tip?"

5. Ask your interviewer to end with a question that leads right into the topic of the workshop such as:

    "What is one expectation you have for this workshop?"

6. As the preplanned questions are asked, the interviewer might insert an additional one or two based on your responses. The facilitator is free to embellish on any question asked.

Notes to Myself

Let Me Introduce You To. . .

Objectives   To provide pertinent information about the facilitator to the participants

To identify the reasons for offering this particular topic and speaker to this group

Group Size   Any size

Time Required   Two to three minutes

Physical Setting   Chairs facing front

Materials Utilized   The facilitator's biography

Content and Process

1. Well in advance of your program, provide a copy of the following handout on preparing an introduction and your resume or biography to your sponsor, client, or whomever is designated to introduce you. Explain the purpose of these instructions and encourage him/her to follow these steps in preparing your introduction.

2. You could also include an actual introduction you have prepared following these same guidelines. Most likely, the person introducing you will use it as is. Refer to the sample introduction that follows.

3. Bring along a copy of the introduction you have prepared just in case the person who is to introduce you forgets his/hers.

4. Stand or sit within view of your participants while you are being introduced so they can visually absorb you as they hear more about you.

Preparing an Introduction

As the program sponsor, you play a key role in getting the program off the ground with an interesting, pertinent, and short introduction of (insert facilitator's name).

A good introduction answers three questions: Why is this facilitator speaking to our group, on this particular topic, at this particular time? Keep these questions in mind as you prepare the introduction, using the information provided in the attached biography plus what you know about your own group members.

1. Why have you chosen _____ as your presenter? Which of her/his credentials should be included in order to build credibility with your group?

2. Why was _____ chosen to do this (workshop, program, speech) with our organization? Has she/he (spoken, presented workshops) with other people with backgrounds similar to ours?

3. Why is the topic of this program appropriate for our group, especially at this particular time?

Sample Introduction

Here is an example of an introduction that answers the three questions.

Introduction of Lois B. Hart

Topic of Program: "Learning From Conflict"

"Like taxes, we can't avoid conflicts. However, we can learn how to manage them better, be more comfortable with those we must face, and use appropriate skills to resolve them.

We have asked Dr. Lois B. Hart to prepare this workshop for us because we appear to have many unresolved conflicts both among ourselves and with some of our customers. We decided that it was time to learn more about how conflicts occur and acquire better methods for resolving our conflicts and learning from them.

Lois has thoroughly studied conflict and has written a book titled, *Learning From Conflict*. She frequently presents workshops and speeches on this topic for organizations very much like ours such as _____ (name a few other clients).

Lois, we are pleased that you are here to help us learn from our conflicts."

Notes to Myself

Ask Me

Objectives   To let participants learn what they need to know about the facilitator

Group Size   Any size

Time Required   Ten minutes

Physical Setting   Tables and chairs facing the front

Materials Utilized   Copies of facilitator's biography (or resume)

Content and Process

1. Distribute your biography or resume as the participants arrive and ask them to look it over while they are waiting for others to arrive.

2. Once the group has assembled, ask the participants to read your biography and underline any facts that intrigue them. For example, someone might notice that the facilitator once worked for the same company or lived in the same city as the participant.

3. Next each person thinks of a question to ask the facilitator that expands upon what he/she just read.

4. Call for volunteers to ask their questions.

5. Once a particular topic is raised, ask if anyone else has a question on the same topic. This way you will not be jumping around but can focus on various aspects of your background.

Notes to Myself

2

Clarifying Expectations and Objectives

The activities in this chapter will help the participants in several ways. Some will help them to clarify the expectations they have about the upcoming learning experience. Others will help them to identify their feelings about being here. Some will help participants to identify their specific needs (here you can suggest how your program may be able to meet these needs). In some cases, participants are asked to identify what resources they can bring to this group experience.

In many of the activities you, as the facilitator, can clarify your own expectations, your program's objectives and design, plus any ground rules you would like the group to follow.

Additional activities that fit the purposes of this chapter but are found elsewhere in this book are:

Welcome to the Workshop

Objectives   To learn, prior to the workshop, the participants' expectations and to use this information in planning the program

To identify participants' needs, questions, and issues

To identify resources participants have that can be useful in the workshop

Group Size   Any size

Time Required   Fifteen to thirty minutes

Physical Setting   Any setting

Materials Utilized   Prepare a letter or questionnaire based on the following instructions.

Content and Process

1. During your planning stage, develop a list of questions that you might ask the participants prior to the workshop that would help you to finalize your workshop design.

2. Prepare a letter/questionnaire that contains a welcoming statement and explanation for the questions that follow. Leave sufficient space for answers.

Questions you might include are:

a. "I chose to attend this workshop because. . ."

b. "Some issues, topics, questions, or skills I would like this workshop to cover are. . ."

c. "I hope this workshop does not. . ."

d. "As a result of this workshop, I hope to be able to. . ."

e. "Resources I could bring to the workshop (books, skills, musical instruments, etc.) include. . ."

f. "Previous experience I have had as a _____ . . ." (Insert the role as it relates to your workshop topic such as supervisor, manager, or administrative assistant.)

3. Include the date by which you need the responses. Indicate where the questionnaire should be returned and/or send the letter/questionnaire with an addressed, stamped return envelope.

Variations/ Comments

• Depending on your specific needs, you could add other questions such as: "How did you find out about this workshop?" or, "What other workshops or courses have you had on this topic?"

• Rather than open-ended questions, you could prepare a list of skills to be acquired and ask the participants to rank them on a scale of 1-5 in terms of their importance to the participant.

Notes to Myself

Objectives and Guidelines

Objectives
To clarify the objectives and guidelines you have established for the workshop

To allow participants to respond to your objectives and guidelines

Group Size
Any size

Time Required
Fifteen minutes

Physical Setting
Any setting

Materials Utilized
Develop a worksheet listing your own objectives and guidelines or use the sample that follows.

Content and Process

1. Prepare a worksheet as shown in the following sample. Add your objectives. Determine the guidelines you will be following to ensure a successful workshop.

2. At the beginning of your workshop, distribute the worksheet and go over your objectives. Give the participants time to respond and then to complete the section listing their personal objectives.

3. Review your objectives and guidelines and your rationale for each. Give the participants a chance to respond and to negotiate changes as needed. An example of a ground rule that often needs discussion is permission for smoking in the meeting room.

4. At the end of the workshop (or periodically if your program runs more than one day), allow time to review the worksheet, noting the objectives that were met. Help the participants determine how unmet objectives could be met through other workshops, courses, books, or people.

Variations/ Comments Create a reusable poster listing your "House Rules." Sketch the outline of a house in the background.

Notes to Myself

Objectives and Suggestions for a Successful Workshop

Today's Objectives Include:

1.

2.

3.

4.

5.

My Own Objectives Include:

1.

2.

3.

4.

5.

Today's Guidelines Include:

1. You are responsible for your own learning. . .so be honest with yourself and ask for what you need.

2. Be as open as possible but you have the right to pass and to privacy.

3. We will respect differences. Be supportive rather than judgmental.

4. Within our group we have all the resources we need to solve any problem that arises.

5. Make at least one new acquaintance today—someone you will contact later on.

6. The program will begin and end on time. We will have frequent breaks but feel free to take care of your physical needs without waiting for a formal break.

7. There will be no smoking in the meeting room.

8. All the materials you receive were prepared for your use. Freely use the hand-outs for note-taking.

9. The evaluation form provides me with useful feedback. Look it over now and add comments to it throughout the day.

Notes to Myself

Why Are You Here?

Objectives   To identify participants' expectations for the workshop

To ensure that the needs that cannot be met with your planned design will be met in other ways

Group Size   Any size

Time Required   Thirty minutes

Physical Setting   Round tables for four to eight people

Materials Utilized   Newsprint, magic markers, tape

Content and Process

1. Divide the total group into smaller groups of four to eight.

2. Each small group should list its members' expectations and specific goals for attending this workshop.

3. Each small group selects a spokesperson who will read and explain its list to the total group.

4. As expectations and goals are read, be sure to indicate which ones will be met with the planned workshop. Goals that cannot be met should not be ignored. You and the participants can identify some ways in which these goals could be met, such as: 1) meet over lunch with someone from this group who has dealt with that problem; 2) suggest a book, course, or other workshop/ seminar.

Notes to Myself

The Whip

Objectives To identify quickly the participants' expectations

Group Size Up to twenty-five participants per facilitator is best, although it could be used in smaller groups of eight to ten without a facilitator

Time Required Thirty seconds per participant

Physical Setting Circle of chairs

Materials Utilized None

Content and Process

1. Explain that we all come to a new workshop with our own set of expectations. Give some examples such as, "I expect peace and quiet with no phones ringing or other interruptions."

2. Ask each person to think silently of one expectation she/he came with today.

3. Starting with the facilitator, each person verbally completes the sentence stem, "My expectation for today's workshop is. . ."

4. Do not ask for explanations. Allow people to pass.

5. Summarize what you have heard from the participants and state which expectations will be met in this workshop. Indicate how the other expectations may be met by suggesting other resources or your availability during meals, breaks, and after the session.

Variations/ Comments

Other sentence stems you could use for this purpose are:

- "My personal goal for the workshop is. . ."
- "I hope. . ."
- "What I can contribute to the workshop is. . ."

You could also select a sentence stem that ties directly into the workshop's content, such as:

- "The most effective leader I've known is. . ."
- "One thing I like about being a supervisor is. . ."

Notes to Myself

The Magic Present

Objectives	To help participants clarify their own expectations and also those of their group
Group Size	Up to thirty participants
Time Required	Thirty minutes
Physical Setting	Circle of chairs
Materials Utilized	One box wrapped up as a present; flipchart or chalkboard
Content and Process	1. Begin by stating how we often come to workshops with unstated wishes for what will happen while we are there. Give some examples: "I wish I could be a better leader" or, "I wish I knew how to deal with my boss."
	2. Show the wrapped box and explain how it is a magic present. Indicate that as the box is passed around the circle, each person is to hold it briefly and make a wish out loud. Post the wishes on a flipchart or board.
	3. As the box goes around, allow people to pass if they appear uncomfortable, but ask them to make their wish silently. Do not allow discussion or judgment of anything that is stated.
	4. Divide the total group into smaller groups of four to five people. The task of each small group is to decide on one wish for the total group.
	5. With the total group, share and post each small group's wish for the total group. Relate these wishes to your objectives for the workshop.

Notes to Myself

Where Would You Rather Be?

Objectives To dispel participants' feelings of either being forced to attend this workshop or wishing they were elsewhere

To help participants identify how they can use this workshop time most effectively

Group Size Any size

Time Required Fifteen to thirty minutes

Physical Setting Small groups of chairs, preferably without tables

Materials Utilized None

Content and Process

1. Explain the purpose of this activity and the process you will use. Ask the participants to get into a comfortable position, either in their chairs or on the floor, and then to close their eyes.

2. Slowly lead them through the following fantasy:

   a. In your mind, go to the place you would rather be at this moment. Look around. Take in what you like about that place.

   b. Now recreate the scene with your boss or other person who compelled you to attend this workshop. How did you feel then? How do you feel now?

   c. Next, mentally go to your place of work—your office or desk area—and review all of the tasks left on your "To Do" list. How do you feel?

  d. Return to the place you would rather be. Look around and decide what is there that you could bring to the present and to this workshop.

  e. Return again to the place of your unfinished demands. Review the expectations others had for you attending this workshop and the unfinished tasks you left behind. Choose one task you could work on today.

3. Ask the participants to open their eyes.

4. Form small groups of three to four people. In these groups, have them share their fantasies, especially the goals that will make the workshop more meaningful for them.

5. In the total group, poll some of the participants' goals. Relate these goals to the objectives and topics of your workshop.

Variations/ Comments

- You could skip the small group sharing if your group is small.

- In Step 5, your discussion could include how they might deal with others who do not want to be at work.

- Instead of a guided fantasy, ask them to record their answers on paper for sharing with their group.

Notes to Myself

Folding Arms

Objectives	To demonstrate how difficult it is to change behavior
Group Size	Any size
Time Required	Ten minutes
Physical Setting	For a small group, use a circle of chairs so the participants can see each other easily
Materials Utilized	None
Content and Process	

1. Ask everyone to fold their arms naturally. Demonstrate.

2. Do a tally of how many fold their arms with:
   - the right hand peeking out
   - the left hand peeking out
   - both hands showing
   - both hands hidden.

3. Ask everyone to refold their arms in the opposite position.

4. Ask for feedback as to how the new position feels. Responses will probably include, "It feels awkward," or "I had to think hard to fold my arms in the new position."

5. Relate the experience to the topic of your workshop. Make the point that change is awkward and we must be patient with ourselves if we are attempting to make either attitudinal or behavioral changes. Encourage the participants to set realistic expectations for themselves.

6. A second point you can make is how we approach problems. We may be set in our ways of folding arms and in our ways of solving problems. To solve problems, we will need to seek alternatives.

Notes to Myself

Issues and Obstacles

Objectives

To help group members who know each other or work together to identify the issues and obstacles that need to be worked on during the workshop

To encourage more active participation and individual responsibility to solve problems

Group Size

Divide total group into small groups of six to eight

Time Required

Thirty to forty-five minutes

Physical Setting

Tables and chairs for six to eight people

Materials Utilized

Newsprint and markers or chalkboard; copies of handout

Content and Process

1. Form groups of six to eight people.

2. Explain that existing issues and obstacles must be recognized if the workshop is to be most effective. Tie this objective into your workshop objectives.

3. Give all participants a copy of the handout that follows and ask them to complete their copy silently.

4. Allow about fifteen minutes to compare notes with their group on the issues and obstacles they have individually identified. Indicate you will be asking for a group report when the time is up.

5. Lead a discussion with the total group. Ask for reports from each small group. As issues and obstacles are mentioned, list them on newsprint or the chalkboard. If one is mentioned more than once, indicate that also. Tie the issues into your workshop objectives.

6. Ask each person to contract with the group to work on a particular issue. Obtain a public commitment from each person.

Notes to Myself

Issues and Obstacles Worksheet

1. Describe one issue that causes you the most difficulty in this group (or in your workgroup). To help you decide which issue is primary, think about a problem that raises feelings of anger, sadness, or frustration or the one that consumes most of your energy.

2. Often we do not move towards a solution because we think other people, their attitudes, or behaviors are the cause for inaction. List the people, circumstances, and events over which you have no control and thus keep you from moving towards a solution.

3. In order to move towards a solution, you must take responsibility for your own action (or inaction), your behaviors, and feelings. Using "I" statements, write down what you are doing, not doing, and feeling that is keeping you from working on the primary issue.

Notes to Myself

3

Who Are You?

The activities in this chapter are used to help reveal information about the participants' own uniqueness, values, ideas, interests, and experiences. This information can be used by them to determine what they need to obtain from this learning experience and from others in the group. These activities also help the facilitator to know the participants better so the presentation can be adapted to fit their needs.

You Ought to Be in Pictures!

Objectives To gather some useful information so all participants will know each other better

Group Size For a short program, this works best with fewer than twenty-five people; for a week-long program, you could do this with up to fifty people

Time Required Thirty minutes

Physical Setting Large space on a wall for posting worksheets

Materials Utilized Prepare a worksheet like the sample; Polaroid camera and sufficient film; glue and tape

Content and Process

1. As participants register, take their photo with the Polaroid camera. Give them a worksheet. Ask them to glue their photo in the appropriate space and to answer the questions.

2. Post the sheets on the wall with the tape.

3. Either during the workshop warm-up or during the breaks, ask the participants to look over the posted sheets, start to place names with faces, and note common interests.

4. Use the information as a means of re-grouping the participants.

5. Copies of the worksheets could be made for participants to keep.

Variations/ Comments

- Ask the participants to complete the worksheet before arriving and to attach a favorite photo.

- Vary the questions to fit the theme, objectives, and content of your workshop.

Notes to Myself

You Ought to Be in Pictures!

Name_____

Nickname _____

Organization _____

Address _____

_____ Phone _____

Position _____

Responsibilities _____

_____

_____

```
┌─────────────┐
│             │
│             │
│             │
│    Photo    │
│             │
│             │
│             │
└─────────────┘
```

What is something exciting that you have done or that has happened to you this past year?

What are your expectations for this workshop?

What resources, skills, and talents do you have that others might enjoy or from which they might benefit?

What unfulfilled dream do you have?

What else would you like us to know about you?

Notes to Myself

The Exhibit Hall

Objectives   To provide a method for getting acquainted and sharing resources

To demonstrate that everyone is an expert at something

Group Size   At least fifteen people

Time Required   Thirty minutes to one hour

Physical Setting   Ample wall space; tables and chairs arranged for easy movement of people to view exhibits

Materials Utilized   Tables with cloths; poster board and markers for signs; name tags with "Exhibitor" ribbons attached

Content and Process

1. When participants preregister, instruct them to bring items that would make up an exhibit based on their experience or skills. Examples include:
   a. A collection of articles/books on a topic that was useful to them
   b. A sample tool kit for home or office
   c. Several performance evaluation forms they have used or found
   d. A step-by-step approach to writing reports
   e. "My best idea for. . ." (written description)
   f. Demonstration on how to. . .

2. Upon arrival at the session, give each person a name tag with an "Exhibitor" ribbon attached. Assign them a table or wall space for their exhibit. Give them materials to make an exhibit sign that identifies their exhibit and shows their name and organizational affiliation.

3. When all of the exhibits are set up, allow time for people to mingle in the Exhibit Hall. Suggest they take paper and pencil for noting exhibits of interest and names for later contact.

Notes to Myself

Resume

Objectives To have participants share some information about their backgrounds

Group Size Any size

Time Required Thirty minutes

Physical Setting Tables and chairs; open space for milling about; flipchart; markers

Materials Utilized Prepare an 8-1/2" x 11" handout with the following information on it and sufficient space for the participants to write in answers.

Resume
Name   Nickname
Current Position
Organization
Educational Background
Other Work Experience
Special Hobbies and Interests
One Positive Experience I Have Had During the Past Month
One Work Problem I Had That is Still Unresolved

Content and Process

1. State that we all come to workshops with a variety of experiences and concerns, many of which we have in common. Pass out the Resume worksheet and ask them to complete each section.

2. Ask them to move into the open space with their Resumes and mill around, greeting new people and sharing the information on their Resumes.

3. After about fifteen minutes and after participants have met at least five new people, ask them to return to their seats (or form new groups).

4. Poll the participants on the kinds of concerns they have, listing these on the flipchart. Relate these concerns to your workshop objectives.

5. Periodically and especially at the end of the program, refer back to the list of concerns, marking off those that were covered and indicating resources that will help people deal with the others.

Variations/ Comments

Change the categories to fit the topic of your workshop or to tap into the interests of your particular group of people.

Notes to Myself

The Name Tag

Objectives   To help participants quickly learn about each other

To re-group participants

Group Size   Any size

Time Required   Thirty to sixty minutes

Physical Setting   Open space for milling about

Materials Utilized   5" x 7" cards; flipchart; overhead projector; markers

Content and Process

1. Before the workshop decide on four categories of information that fit your workshop topic and what you know about the participants. Choose from the categories provided with this exercise.

2. Explain the purpose of the workshop. Hand out the cards that have been printed as shown below, or have participants draw similar spaces on a blank card to be used as a name tag.

Name:	

3. Introduce one category at a time, posting the category information on a flipchart or transparency. Reassure the participants that they do not have to complete all information; they can come back to it later.

4. When all four blocks are completed, ask everyone to stand and move into the open space. Ask them to mill around, holding their name tags in front of them so others can read them. They may make comments, ask questions, and exchange information. Encourage them to keep moving until they have met ten to fifteen people (everyone if the group is small).

5. While they are still standing, get their attention and ask them to form small groups of five or six (perhaps selecting those whom they found interesting during the milling process).

6. When the small groups are formed, make sure they introduce themselves. Then with the new group, discuss each other's expectations and concerns or a question related to the topic of the workshop.

7. With the total group, discuss their experiences getting acquainted, especially how that relates to the responsibility they have to help others become integrated into an existing group. Poll them for their concerns and expectations.

Notes to Myself

Examples of Categories
for the Name Tag

Characteristics
As a leader, what characteristics do you like. . .
    in your followers?
    in your colleagues?
    in your boss?

What characteristics do you like. . .
    in a lover?
    in a friend?
    in a parent?
    in a child?

Dates
Of your greatest love
Of time of greatest changes or painful events in your life
Of your greatest summer
Of your most rewarding job
When you finally "grew up"

Expectations
List three expectations you have for this workshop.

Future
If you had one year off with no financial worries or other
    responsibilities, what would you do?
What do you want to be doing in five years?
What is your greatest concern for the future of your organ-
    ization (nation or world)?

Intense Moments
A time you cried your hardest
The time you laughed the most
A time you were close to dying or were with someone who
    almost died

Motivation
List three things or conditions that motivate you to do your
    very best.

People
A person who influenced your life
A person you enjoy being around
Someone you admire
Three effective leaders

Personal Qualities	List three qualities that best describe you. List three strengths that will help you to achieve your goals. List up to three qualities that you would like to develop further. Write three words by which you would like to be remembered.
Places	Where you were born The place you were the happiest A place you would like to live (perhaps where you live now)
Problems	List three problems or concerns you hope will be resolved during the workshop.
Roles/ Aspirations	A role you have aspired to A role given to you that you do not like A role you enjoy Title of current work role
Special Interest and Hobbies	Name your favorite hobby or interest as a teenager. List up to three of your favorite hobbies today. List one activity you like to do alone and one you like to do with others.
Success	A childhood success A success in the past five years A success in the past month
Support/ Trust	Name the place you go (or have gone) where you feel "safe" and "secure." Name the time or event when you received just the right amount of support. Name one person whom you trust or is especially supportive.
Teaching and Learning	Who is someone who taught you a lot? List the qualities of an effective teacher/trainer. What qualities do you like in your learner?
Values	What are three values you hold dearly, are willing to tell others about, and would defend?

The People Hunt

Objectives
To provide an opportunity for groups of people to become acquainted or reacquainted

To increase the level of comfort among strangers

To examine one's feelings when forced to meet new people

Group Size
A minimum of twenty; this activity works well with hundreds of people

Time Required
Thirty minutes for instructions and milling time; more if followed up with small group discussions

Physical Setting
A large open space for milling about

Materials Utilized
A hand-mike for groups over thirty; pens/pencils

Prepare a handout or 5" x 7" card with ten to fifteen key items selected from the following examples. Card stock is easier to write on and hold when milling about.

Content and Process

1. There are two ways to introduce this activity; choose the one that fits your purpose. You can distribute the cards as people register and have them start to mingle immediately, or you can wait until everyone has arrived to start the exercise.

2. Explain the purpose of the activity. Let them read the directions and skim the items. Have the entire group standing before they begin to exchange information.

3. Every few minutes remind them they should be moving along to meet new people. You could suggest a minimum number of people with whom they should talk.

4. When the time is up, either have them return to their seats or form new groups.

5. Process the experience with them. If you have formed small groups, have them discuss the following in their groups first, and later summarize with the total group. Questions include:

   a. What was the most interesting bit of information you learned about another person?

   b. Which information was easiest and which was hardest to give out to others?

   c. Which information was easiest and hardest to ask others?

   d. How can we help ourselves and others become comfortable more quickly when we are in new groups of people?

6. Suggest the participants keep the names of those people they met during the activity and make arrangements to continue developing the relationships during breaks or after the session.

Sample Instructions

The following are examples of instructions you might use.

1. "The purpose of this activity is for you to catch up on what has been happening in the lives of those people whom you already know and to get acquainted with some you do not know. Try to match up people with most of the categories listed below. You must actually speak to people—do not use prior knowledge. Put the name or initials of each person next to the category they match. You have thirty minutes to do this."

— or —

2. "The purpose of this activity is for you to gain an unusual insight into the lives of the others at this workshop. Find a person who matches each description listed below. Put his/her name next to the matching category. You have thirty minutes to do this."

Examples

1. Here are some categories you could use directly or adapt to fit your workshop objectives and what you know about your participants. Use no more than fifteen items.

Find someone who. . .

_____ can name a hero or heroine who has been a model for them

_____ has heard a joke recently and is willing to share it

_____ took a risk this past week

_____ traveled the farthest to get here

_____ enjoys leadership

_____ has a tip on managing stress

_____ carries at least eight membership cards

_____ aspires to move to the top of his/her organization

_____ is not sure why he/she is here today

_____ is sure why he/she is here today

_____ has a Susan B. Anthony dollar with him/her

_____ played a "power game" and won

_____ feels great

_____ needs a "shot in the arm"

_____ has blue eyes

_____ has the same astrological sign as you do

_____ traveled to another country for vacation

_____ shares the same hobby as you do

_____ has given up a habit recently

_____ had a "first" this year

_____ had a child born or adopted into his/her family this last year

_____ had a child move out this year

_____ got married or divorced this year

_____ was born in the same city or town as you were

_____ knows where the bathrooms are

_____ had a success recently

_____ has written a book

_____ wants to write a book

_____ needs a backrub

_____ recently fought a consumer battle

_____ talks to his/her houseplants

_____ had a conflict already today

2. The following is an example of how to word your categories to fit the content of a workshop, in this case a workshop on decision making.

Find someone who. . .

_____ recently made a last-minute decision they now regret

_____ recently made a last-minute decision that worked

_____ likes to make decisions alone

_____ prefers to involve others in their decision making

_____ makes decisions better in the morning

_____ makes decisions better in the afternoon

_____ can define the word "consensus"

_____ has a favorite saying that guides their decision making

Notes to Myself

What's in Your Wallet or Purse?

Objectives	To get acquainted in a nonthreatening way
Group Size	Up to twenty participants; if more, form additional circles
Time Required	Fifteen minutes
Physical Setting	Circle of chairs
Materials Utilized	None

Content and Process

1. Participants form a circle of chairs.

2. Participants select one item from their wallet or purse that reveals something about themselves or is something they are proud of. They will share with the group why they selected that item.

3. The leader starts with his/her own item.

4. Proceed around the circle until everyone has had a chance to share.

Variations/ Comments

Select an item you are wearing and talk about it.

Notes to Myself

Where Are You From?

Objectives   To help participants learn something unique about each other

To help participants relax

Group Size   Optimum is thirty unless you use the variation

Time Required   Fifteen minutes

Physical Setting   Large open space

Materials Utilized   Make large paper signs for each of the major regions of the United States, plus one labeled "Other Countries." The regions could be: Northeast, Southeast, Midwest, Mountain States, Far West, Southwest, Alaska, Hawaii.

Content and Process

1. Lay the regional signs on the floor, ideally in the approximate configuration of the U.S.

2. Ask the participants to stand on or near the sign that identifies where they were born. Let participants discuss details with the others standing on the same sign.

3. Next, have everyone move to the region where they live now. Have them discuss how they happened to move to this place or why they remained in the place of their birth.

4. Now, ask everyone to move to the region that represents the ideal place to live or the place where they may have dreamed about living. Ask them to explain.

5. Discuss what they left behind when they moved to their most recent location.

6. Depending on your objectives, either have the participants return to their seats or form new groups.

7. Discuss how the places we were born, grew up, and currently live in affect our view of life, work, and relationships. Tie this into the content of your workshop.

Variations/ Comments

Post a large map of the United States or the world on the wall. As participants register, have them place their name on a small slip of paper (or a Post-It) and pin it to the spot on the map where they were born (or currently live). Use this information to form new groups.

Notes to Myself

My Personal Shield

Objectives   To have participants share some information about their backgrounds, values, and philosophy of life

Group Size   Any size; groups of five to six participants will be formed

Time Required   Thirty minutes

Physical Setting   Tables and chairs

Materials Utilized   Plain 8-1/2" x 11" paper; pencils; flipchart (or chalkboard); markers

Content and Process

1. Form groups of five to six participants per table. Explain the purpose of the activity. Distribute one piece of paper and a pencil per participant.

2. Draw a shield on the flipchart (or chalkboard) that looks like the shield provided with this exercise. Ask the participants to draw the same shield on their paper. It should fill the 8-1/2" x 11" sheet.

3. Ask them to write their responses to the following six questions in the corresponding numbered space on their shields. Give them one question at a time and allow about two minutes to write each response.

4. When the six questions have been answered, ask the participants to write wherever there is blank space, "your personal motto by which you try to live."

5. Have the participants share this information verbally with their group by giving their response to each question and elaborating on the response. This can be accomplished by each individual revealing his/her entire shield, or by the group members each responding in turn to question one, then each responding to question two, and so forth.

6. Allow about fifteen minutes for this activity.

7. Lead a short discussion on how our backgrounds, values, and philosophies affect how we interact and work. Tie what is shared into the content of your workshop.

Questions

1. The greatest joy of my life is. . .

2. The most important decision I ever made was. . .

3. My constant worry is. . .

4. As a child, I dreamed of. . .

5. The thing I love most about life is. . .

6. What I would like to change in my life is. . .

Notes to Myself

My Personal Shield

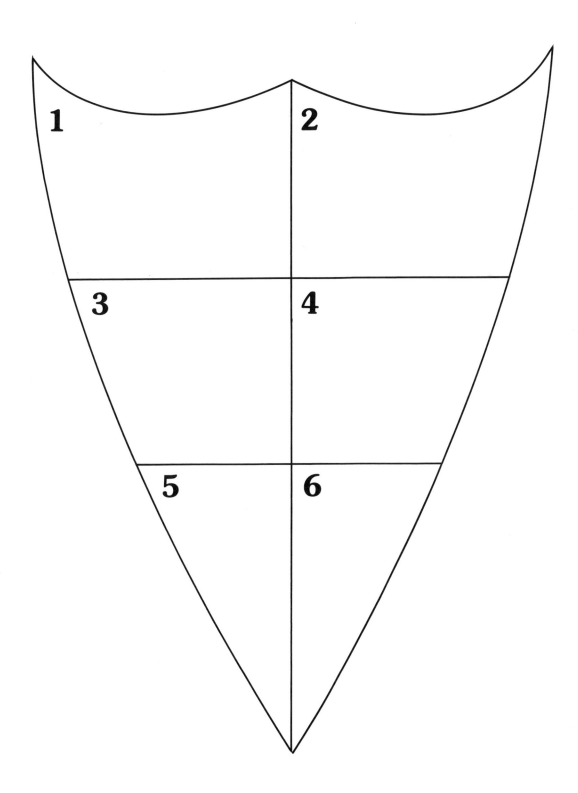

Notes to Myself

Here's My Card

Objectives   To help participants get acquainted with one another

To emphasize the importance of having and using business cards

Group Size   Any size

Time Required   Thirty to sixty minutes

Physical Setting   Open space for milling about; tables and chairs

Materials Utilized   Colored pencils; samples of several business cards

Prepare 5-1/2" x 8" stock weight cards and print one side with the questions you want answered by the participants. Use the questions from Step 4 of this exercise or develop your own. Leave spaces for responses.

Content and Process

1. Ask, "How many of you carry business cards?" Ask them to take them out. Ask, "How many of you had the chance to design your own?"

2. Explain the purpose of this activity. Talk about why people use business cards and how they symbolize who we are or where we work. Together look over sample business cards and discuss their perceptions of the different logos.

3. Distribute your cards and pencils. Direct their attention to the blank side of the card. Explain that they have the opportunity to create their own card. Give them time to create their own card, including the basic information of name, address, phone number, and title. Encourage them to create a logo or design that symbolizes who they are or what they do.

4. Next, direct the participants' attention to the sentence stems on the other side of their card. Ask them to complete each sentence. For example, if you were teaching a supervisory course, sentence stems might be:

   a. "What I like best about my job is. . ."

   b. "The best supervisor I worked for had these characteristics:"

   c. "Qualities I do not like in a supervisor are:"

   d. "I do (or do not) like supervising others because. . ."

5. After the participants have designed their cards and completed the sentence stems, ask them to move into the open area with their cards. They are to mingle, shaking hands with at least five new people and sharing information on their cards or explaining their logo or card design.

6. After about fifteen minutes, re-group participants into small groups and ask them to review what they have found out about each other. Use this information to assess their needs and tie these needs into the objectives of your workshop.

Notes to Myself

What's in a Name?

Objectives   To learn something unique about each other

To increase participants' level of comfort with the other group members

Group Size   Any size

Time Required   Fifteen minutes

Physical Setting   Small groups of chairs

Materials Utilized   None

Content and Process

1. Form groups of three to five people.

2. Introduce the idea that many of us have a story behind our names. Tell the story of your name.

3. Ask participants to take about two minutes each to tell their name stories in their small group. Include how they got their name, whom they were named after, or other bits of information.

4. Next, ask them to share the name they would rather have, if they could.

5. Have each person indicate what they want to be called during the workshop.

Variations/
Comments

- Ask people with the same first name to gather together and discuss their perceptions of their name.

- Use a letter of each person's name as a means of re-grouping participants: either all with the same first initial or in groups based on the four parts of the alphabet, A-F, G-L, M-R, and S-Z (by first or last name).

- Each person thinks of a series of physical movements that fit the number of syllables in his/her name; for example, Lois has two syllables and could be represented by a two-movement hand salute. Give everyone time to plan the distinct and repeatable movements that fit his/her name. Demonstrate with yours first. Continue around the group until everyone has had a chance to demonstrate and lead others in his/her name cheer.

Notes to Myself

Name Your Uniqueness

Objectives   To have participants learn each others' names and something unique about each person

To relax participants

Group Size   Up to twenty-five people; if a larger group, form several
circles

Time Required   Fifteen minutes

Physical Setting A circle of chairs or open space large enough to form a
circle with everyone standing

Materials Utilized None

Content and Process

1. Form a circle, either with chairs or standing.

2. Explain how we all have self-perceptions that sometimes take awhile to reveal to others. Although our
   negative self-perceptions often dominate, the purpose
   here is to share a positive one with the other group
   members.

3. Ask participants to think of an adjective that they could
   put in front of their names. They may fracture the lan-
   guage a bit to do this. Examples are:

   "I'm lively Lois."
   "I'm enthusiastic Ed."
   "I'm reflective Arn."
   "I'm questioning Sue."

4. Start by giving your own name and adjective. Each person in turn gives his/hers. Go slowly so everyone can absorb impressions.

5. If time allows, form groups of five to six people and have them briefly explain why they chose their adjective.

Variations/ Comments

- You could combine this activity with "First Impressions."

- A more difficult version would be to have each person select a superlative relative to the other group members, such as "tallest, smallest feet, most anxious, most shy. . ."

Notes to Myself

First Impressions

Objectives
To have participants share their first impressions of each other

To recognize the dangers of acting only on first impressions

Group Size
Up to thirty people

Time Required
Forty-five minutes

Physical Setting
Open space for milling about

Materials Utilized
1" x 1" gummed labels; 5" x 7" cards

Prepare a transparency, flipchart sheet, or handout of the list of characteristics provided with this exercise (or devise your own list).

Content and Process

1. Form a circle. Ask the participants to move their eyes around the circle, looking at each person and registering their first impressions. Do this without any talking.

2. Next, ask everyone to slowly mill about, shaking hands with everyone they meet and giving a friendly greeting.

3. Next, ask them to share one bit of information with each person they meet, such as where they work, their hobby, or favorite food.

4. Then, distribute ten gummed labels and one 5" x 7" card to each person. Show them the list of characteristics either on the flipchart, overhead projector, or on a handout. Ask them to continue milling about, but now when they stop before each person, they are to write on a label one characteristic that best describes the person they are viewing, and stick that label on the person's card. Ask them to do this with a minimum of conversation.

5. Have the participants move on until each person has received ten labels.

6. Form small groups and discuss the following:
   a. How did you feel being asked to tell others your first impressions of them?
   b. Of the labels given to you, which were the most accurate? Least accurate?
   c. What are the dangers of first impressions?
   d. How can we use first impressions more positively?

7. Ask for a few sample reactions to share with the total group.

Variations/ Comments

- An extension of this activity would be in-depth interviewing and sharing of personal information.

- Instead of providing the list of characteristics, participants could use their own words.

- Instead of using labels, give participants paper and colored markers or crayons. In dyads, ask them to sketch something representative of their partner based on what they learned while milling about.

- Allow time at the end of the workshop for participants to rewrite their impressions of each other.

Examples of Characteristics

happy	sad	friendly
mellow	anxious	aloof
fatherly	motherly	sisterly
brotherly	sexy	fun
mysterious	warm	pensive
creative	colorful	enthusiastic

Notes to Myself

Post It

Objectives   To have participants reveal something about themselves

Group Size   Up to thirty people

Time Required   Fifteen to thirty minutes

Physical Setting   One blank wall for Post-Its; chairs

Materials Utilized   Several packages of 3" x 3" Post-Its

Content and Process

1. Give each person six Post-Its. Ask them to write on each Post-It one characteristic that describes themselves. Keep the characteristics general. Do not sign. Examples might include: happy, good supervisor, self-disciplined, creative.

2. Have everyone stick their Post-Its on the designated wall. Allow time for participants to look over the Post-Its to see similarities and differences of self-perceptions.

3. Ask each person to select a Post-It that identifies a characteristic they would like to have that they do not have now.

4. Form groups of five to six people. Ask the participants to reveal to their group the characteristic they selected, and explain why they selected it.

Notes to Myself

The Picket Line

Objectives   To let participants get acquainted in a playful manner

To have participants learn more about each other

Group Size   This activity works well with as few as ten people or with large groups

Time Required   Thirty minutes

Physical Setting   Tables and chairs for Steps 1-4; large open space for Step 5

Materials Utilized   12" x 18" poster boards in several colors—two per person; markers or crayons in many colors; string; hole punch

Content and Process

1. Distribute two pieces of poster board per person. Let them choose the colors that appeal to them, both in poster board and markers/crayons.

2. Ask them to think of something that symbolizes who they are, what they value, an achievement, a special interest, or a hobby. Give them time to think. Have them draw their symbol on one of the poster boards.

3. Now ask them to think of a phrase, key word, or sentence that represents them, such as "I'm a winner," or "Fight, fight, win!" or "Always love," or "See, then do." They are to write their words on the second poster board.

4. Use the hole punch and string to make picket signs. Connect the two signs, one below the other, and use a large loop of string to hang the double sign around their necks.

5. Participants put on their picket signs and mingle in the open space, stopping to ask each other questions, make comments, and learn each others' names. Encourage them to meet at least ten new people.

Variations/ Comments

Other drawings or words could be put on the boards such as:

1. A piechart showing how they spend their time.

2. A scene of how they play (on one board) and how they work (on the other board).

3. A sketch of what makes them happiest (on one board) and what makes them most sad (on the other).

Notes to Myself

I See Me As. . .

Objectives To encourage participants to share information about themselves

To identify resources among the group members

Group Size This works well with a large group followed by smaller groups of four to six

Time Required Thirty minutes

Physical Setting Open space for milling about; chairs for small groups

Materials Utilized Put word list on a handout or transparency

3" x 5" cards; pens or pencils

Content and Process

1. Explain the purpose of the activity and the value of revealing information about oneself to others.

2. Either hand out the list of words or show the participants the list on the transparency.

3. Ask the participants to select four words from the list that most closely characterize them and to write them on the card.

4. Next, have everyone mill in the open space. As they make contact with another person, they are to say, "I see me as. . ." and state one of their selected words, and give an example from their work or personal life that demonstrates how they are 'like' the chosen word.

5. Circulate among the participants. Encourage them to talk with at least five to seven people in fifteen minutes.

6. After about fifteen minutes, form groups of four to six people. Have them discuss what they have learned about each other and how they felt during this self-disclosure activity.

7. With the total group, gather information about the participants so a profile can be established. Also gather information on the resources available among the group members.

Variations/ Comments

- Skip the milling about and instead form the small groups immediately.

- The activity works well to build a team, to identify what the members have in common and the resources available among them that can be applied to their work.

- Tie words into the content of your workshop. For example, supervisors and managers can focus on words that are relevant to leadership and authority.

Word List

accurate	attentive	cheerful
daring	dependable	disciplined
flexible	intelligent	optimistic
outgoing	persistent	resourceful
thorough	wise	ambitious
bold	confident	decisive
friendly	orderly	enthusiastic
open-minded	patient	sincere
witty	creative	understanding

Are You More. . .

Objectives   To provide an opportunity for participants to reveal something of themselves

To exemplify desired behaviors as modeled by the facilitator

To re-group participants

Group Size   Fifteen to fifty people

Time Required   Approximately five minutes per pair of items used

Physical Setting   A large open space

Materials Utilized   A microphone for groups over thirty; newsprint; markers

Content and Process

1. Select pairs of items from the samples provided with this exercise. You may not use all of the pairs, but it is good to have them ready. Particularly, select those that pertain to your workshop topic.

2. Explain the purpose of the activity. Tell the participants that you will be giving them pairs of items and they are to decide which item of the pair is more like them. Point out the two places in the room that will be used for the forced choices. There is no middle point; every-one must choose one of the items.

3. Call out your first pair and list one of the item words on newsprint at one end of the room and the second at the other end. Ask participants to move to the end of the room where their item choice is posted.

4. When everyone has moved to the appropriate end of the room, ask them to share with one or two people closest to them the reasons for their choice.

5. After no more than two minutes, lead a discussion between the two groups. Be sure to maintain the rule that this is a time for sharing information, not for arguing or challenging. Questions you might ask are:

   a. Who would give a summary of the reasons people in their group gave for selecting that item?

   b. What questions would you like to ask of anyone at the other end of the room?

   c. What made it hard to decide which position to take?

6. Call out a second pair of items, posting them on newsprint, and ask participants to choose their item and go to the appropriate end of the room. Follow the same procedure.

7. Do as many pairs as you feel the group can handle, time allows, or meets your purposes.

Variations/ Comments   Instead of having people "vote with their feet," prepare a handout of as many pairs as you want. You could use cartoons or pictures illustrating each polarity. After participants select the items that are most like them, form small groups to discuss their choices.

Notes to Myself

Are You More. . .

Sample Pairs or Forced Choices

Are you more. . .

- like a rose or grass?
- like summer or winter?
- like the country or city?
- a leader or a follower?
- physical or mental?
- a tortoise or a hare?
- 1990 or 1790?
- a mountain or a valley?
- a screened porch or a picture window?
- a saver or a spender?
- like morning or night?
- New York City or Laramie, WY?
- the mountains or plains?
- creator or doer?
- left brain or right brain?
- like a paddle or a ping-pong ball?
- a Corvette or a Bronco?
- bubbling brook or placid lake?
- a McDonald's or a French restaurant?
- a loner or a groupee?

Notes to Myself

The Real Me

Objectives	To have participants share information about themselves
Group Size	Any size
Time Required	Thirty minutes
Physical Setting	Tables and chairs
Materials Utilized	The handout, "The Real Me"
Content and Process	1. Prepare a handout like the one shown with this exercise. Distribute the handout and explain the purpose of this activity.
	2. Give the participants about three to five minutes to complete the handout.
	3. Form small groups of three to five people and ask them to share with their group one of the items they have responded to on their handout.
	4. With the total group, solicit volunteers to share any patterns of information the small groups have discovered about themselves.
	5. Tie in these observations to the objectives of your workshop.

The Real Me

Directions   Please take four or five minutes to respond *briefly* to these three statements. In a few minutes, you will be asked to share your responses with your group as a way of getting to know each other at a deeper, more meaningful level.

List two things that are really important to you.

1. _____

2. _____

List two things that you are really proud of in your work.

1. _____

2. _____

List two things that you would like to accomplish in your work during the next three years if your work conditions could be ideal.

1. _____

2. _____

Notes to Myself

You Can't Tell a Book by Its Cover

Objectives
To reveal more about oneself to another participant and in turn learn more about someone else

To help participants relax and prepare for the group experience

Group Size
Any size; pairs are formed

Time Required
Thirty minutes

Physical Setting
Moveable furniture

Materials Utilized
Prepare an 8-1/2" x 11" handout with the image of an "Open Book" on it, using the page lengthwise. Number from 1-4 on the left page and 5-8 on the right page with lines for writing responses.

Newsprint or overhead projector; markers

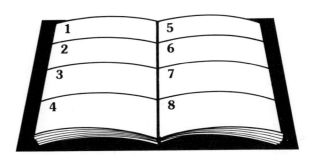

Content and Process
1. Start with a statement about how each of us presents one face to those around us, but behind that "mask" and below our surface is the real person. Often we are judged, like books, on what we show to others. One way we can discover who we really are is to reveal ourselves to others and let them react to us. Explain the value of this kind of disclosure as it relates to the objectives of your workshop.

2. Give each person a copy of the handout. Explain that you will be presenting eight categories of information for them to record in their "Open Book."

3. As you present each of the following categories, list it on newsprint or on a transparency.

    (1) What do you want to be called today?

    (2) What is your favorite time of day?

    (3) How do you like to spend your spare time (the time that is just for you)?

    (4) Write one word to show how you would describe yourself.

    (5) Write one word that others would use to describe you.

    (6) What is one gift you are willing to share with others in this group?

    (7) Name one strength you have.

    (8) Name one thing you value.

4. After the participants have completed their own "Open Book," form dyads and have them share their information.

5. Hold a short review discussion with the total group, gathering observations on what they have discovered about themselves and each other and how this information can be used to enhance the learning in the remainder of the workshop.

Variations/ Comments

- Put the image of an "Open Book" on 5" x 7" cards so they can be worn as name tags.

- Adapt the entries you want for the "Open Book" to fit the content of your workshop and what you know about the participants.

The Movie Screen

Objectives   To learn more about participants' past experiences and their dreams for the future that might affect their learning in this workshop

To have participants get acquainted in a fun manner

Group Size   Any size

Time Required   Thirty minutes

Physical Setting   Tables and chairs

Materials Utilized   Prepare an 8-1/2" x 11" handout that looks like this:

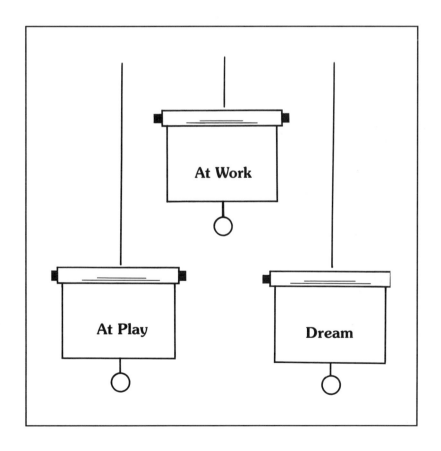

Content and Process

1. Explain that we each come to the workshop with past experiences and future dreams that will affect what we will get from this learning experience.

2. Distribute the "Movie Screen" handout. Ask the participants to draw in the first screen, labeled "At Work," a scene of them that is characteristic of their life at work.

3. In the second screen, have them draw a scene of themselves when they are "At Play."

4. In the third screen, have them draw a scene that represents one dream or fantasy — something they have not yet accomplished.

5. In small groups, participants show their "Movie Screens," sharing more details with the group.

6. Discuss in the total group how our past experiences and dreams for the future can affect the quality of learning that will occur in this workshop.

Notes to Myself

Feelings Wheel

Objectives   To help participants identify their present feelings

   To help the facilitator assess the mood of the group

Group Size   Any size

Time Required   Fifteen to thirty minutes

Physical Setting   Tables and chairs

Materials Utilized   Prepare an 8-1/2" x 11" handout that looks like this:

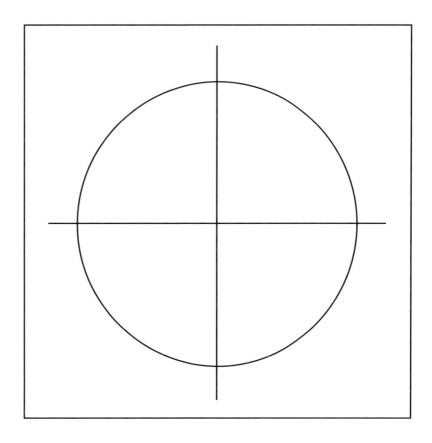

Content and Process

1. Explain that each of us comes to a new workshop with our own set of feelings including ones of anxiety, relief, anticipation, or excitement.

2. Give each person the "Feelings Wheel" handout. Ask them to think of and then write down one feeling in each of the four sections of the wheel. Make a distinction between feelings and thoughts, for example:

Thoughts	Feelings
"I think this group is too big."	"I feel anxious."
"I think I will learn a lot."	"I am excited."
"I think I will enjoy being away from the phone today."	"I am happy."
	"I am nervous."
"I think I would like a break."	"I am optimistic."
"I think I should take a lot of notes."	"I am scared."

3. Next, have each person circle the feeling on the wheel that stands out the most for him/her.

4. In dyads or trios have participants share some of their feelings and the reasons behind them.

Notes to Myself

Meet My Orange

Objectives

To increase awareness of individual differences

To increase use of all the human senses

Group Size

Up to twenty people; if more, create several groups of equal size

Time Required

Thirty minutes

Physical Setting

Chairs; a table

Materials Utilized

One orange per participant

Content and Process

1. Form a large circle. Give an orange to each person.

2. Explain that, like people, no two oranges are alike. Give them two minutes to "get acquainted" with their own orange. Suggest that they study it first with their eyes, then close their eyes and feel it carefully.

3. Form dyads. Individuals are to "introduce" their orange to their partner, pointing out its uniqueness. Suggest they exchange oranges to help "get acquainted" better.

4. Ask the total group to come together again. Collect the oranges, mix them up, and spread them out on a table. Ask the participants to find their own orange again.

5. Ask the participants to take chairs and form groups of four to six to discuss the activity.

6. Use the following questions for discussion:

   a. What were the distinguishing features of your orange?

   b. In what ways are people like oranges?

   c. Because we cannot go around "touching" other people in order to get acquainted, how can we learn about others' uniqueness?

Variations/ Comments   Use apples or unshelled peanuts instead of oranges.

Notes to Myself

4

Who Are We?

The purpose of the activities in this chapter is to help the facilitator and the participants identify what they have in common and how they are different from one another. In these activities, the participants will learn each others' names, their commonalities, and the various roles they hold in life. These activities can also be used to help develop a sense of group teamwork and unity.

Twenty Questions

Objectives	To gather quickly information about group participants
Group Size	Any size
Time Required	Five minutes
Physical Setting	Any setting
Materials Utilized	None
Content and Process	1. Before the workshop, prepare a list of twenty questions based on information you want to obtain about the participants. See the examples included with this exercise.

1. Before the workshop, prepare a list of twenty questions based on information you want to obtain about the participants. See the examples included with this exercise.

2. Explain that you have a list of questions that will help everyone, including you, learn more about "who we are."

3. Ask the participants to move their materials so they can stand easily each time they answer "Yes" to a question. (You could have them raise their hands as an alternative method.)

4. Begin asking the questions. Leave just enough time between them for participants to stand and for everyone to note who has stood.

5. Thank them for their cooperation. Make additional comments if you want to tie the exercise to the content of the workshop.

Sample Questions

1. Who is from (Denver, Chicago, New York, etc.)?
2. Who is a (supervisor, manager, teacher, etc.)?
3. Who would like to take a stretch break?
4. Who has recently read a book or article on (name a topic)?
5. Who has heard me speak before?
6. Who likes to (ski, sail, jog, play tennis, etc.)?
7. Who has had at least one hug today?
8. Who is here with his/her (spouse, boss, colleague, friend)?
9. Who had enough sleep last night?
10. Who is (under thirty; over fifty)?
11. Stand if you are the parent of one child (two, three, etc.).
12. Who traveled 100 miles to get here today (500; 1000)?

Prepare additional questions so there will be a total of twenty. Prepare questions that will tell you what you need to know about the participants or that will tie into the content of your workshop.

Notes to Myself

Around the Circle

Objectives	To help participants quickly learn the names of everyone in the group
	To practice listening and memory skills
Group Size	May be difficult to do with a group of more than twenty people
Time Required	Thirty minutes
Physical Setting	Circle of chairs
Materials Utilized	None

Content and Process

1. Ask participants to remove their name tags or put any name tents away.

2. Discuss the value of learning everyone's names.

3. Indicate that you all will be learning each others' names in the following way: Give your name. The person to your right says, "My name is (gives name) and this is (repeats your name).

4. The process continues on to the right, each person introducing him or herself then repeating back the names of those previously introduced. For example: My name is Lois./My name is Jane and this is Lois./My name is Bob. This is Lois and this is Jane. Etc.

5. Continue until everyone has been named; then as the facilitator, you repeat every participant's name.

Notes to Myself

Name-Go

Objectives	To help participants learn the names of everyone in the group
Group Size	No fewer than nine people nor more than thirty-five
Time Required	Thirty minutes
Physical Setting	Open space for milling about
Materials Utilized	Prepare an 8-1/2" x 11" handout, designing the "Name-Go" card according to the number of people you have. Make the chart fill the page.

For 9-15 People:

For 16-24 People:

For 24-35 People:

Content and Process

1. As participants arrive, give each one a copy of the "Name-Go" handout. Explain that they are to meet the other participants and have each person they greet sign their name in one of the boxes.

2. When everyone has a name in each box, ask them to find a seat.

3. Explain that the next step is like playing "Bingo." As you call each person's name from the registration list, that person stands and players who have that person's name in a square put an X in that square.

4. The first player to get three, four, or five names (depending on the chart used) in a vertical, horizontal, or diagonal row calls out "Name-Go" and wins.

5. Give a prize to the winner(s).

Notes to Myself

How Many Hats Do We Wear?

Objectives

To identify the many roles we play

To help participants see what they have in common

Group Size

Up to twenty people

Time Required

Fifteen minutes

Physical Setting

Circle of chairs

Materials Utilized

None

Content and Process

1. Form a circle of chairs.

2. Make an opening statement about the many roles or "hats" we wear. Explain that you will be naming many situations. The participants are to indicate what role they play in that situation.

3. Start with the sentence stem, "At home, I am a. . .," and ask each person to name a role they play at home such as parent, fixer, cook.

4. Do several rounds using these sentence stems:
   - "At work, I am a. . ."
   - "In my community, I am a. . ."
   - "In this group, I will be a. . ."

5. Invite participants to suggest an additional sentence stem.

Variations/ Comments

Have everyone stand in a circle. Explain that as you name categories/roles, appropriate individuals are to move into the inner circle and briefly discuss what they have in common. Examples are: all men; all women; all leaders; all talkers; all good listeners; all parents. See more examples of categories in the exercise, "Potpourri."

Notes to Myself

What's Your Sign?

Objectives   To learn more about each other in a light-hearted way

To re-group participants

Group Size   This works best for up to fifty people

Time Required   Fifteen to thirty minutes

Physical Setting   Moveable furniture

Materials Utilized   Prepare twelve table-tents out of heavy paper. Label each with an astrological sign. The symbol could also be used. Cut out today's horoscope from the newspaper and tape each sign's information unobtrusively inside the appropriate tent.

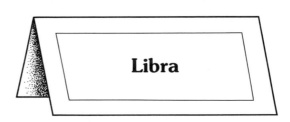

Content and Process

1. Find out if anyone has had a birthday recently. Make a statement about the belief held by many people that the date we were born determines who we are and how we respond to life.

2. Lay the twelve tents out on a table. Ask the participants to find all others in the group who have their same astrological sign, pick up their tent, and re-group accordingly. If there are large numbers of a particular sign, divide that group so there are no more than eight in a group. If there is only one person for a sign, place him/her with the sign closest to his/hers (by date).

3. In their astrological groups, have them discuss:

   a. What do astrologers say is characteristic of their sign? To what degree are the astrologers accurate relative to what the participants know about themselves?

   b. What are the implications for (employees, leaders, parents, spouses) if what is said about people of our sign is true? (For example, suppose your "sign" does not get along well with the one that your boss happens to have?)

4. Indicate that today's horoscope is taped inside the tent. Give them time to read it and react.

5. As a total group, compare notes on what was discussed. Make observations as they relate to your workshop topic. Note, too, which sign solved problems easily, talked more (or less), and disclosed information easily.

Variations/ Comments

- Instead of using astrological signs, groups could be formed based on participants' interests in particular sports, hobbies, home states, or favorite foods.

- Distribute yesterday's horoscope and give them time to react.

Notes to Myself

I'd Like You to Meet

Objectives
To have participants quickly learn more about each other
To practice listening and summarizing skills

Group Size
Any size

Time Required
Thirty minutes

Physical Setting
Moveable chairs

Materials Utilized
None

Content and Process

1. Explain the purpose of the activity.

2. Form dyads of people who do not know each other.

3. In the dyads, each person takes about three to five minutes to talk about himself/herself.

4. Next, have each dyad join another dyad, forming a group of four. Each person introduces his/her partner to the new dyad.

5. In the total group, poll participants to find out what they have learned about one another.

Variations/ Comments

- If your group is fewer than twenty people, you could have the introductions of partners done in the total group.

- Suggest some topics that could be discussed in the dyads. These topics could relate to the content of your workshop.

Notes to Myself

Tell Me More!

Objectives To learn quickly more about the participants

To have participants disclose information about themselves

Group Size Any size

Time Required Thirty minutes

Physical Setting Moveable chairs

Materials Utilized None

Content and Process

1. Form trios of people who do not know each other.

2. Each person in turn tells something about himself/herself or responds to any questions asked of him/her. Limit the disclosure to one piece of information per person.

3. Re-group everyone into new trios. Repeat the process of offering information or answering questions; however, what is told must be new information.

4. Every three to five minutes form new trios and repeat the process. Re-group approximately four times, longer if the group's energy is high.

5. In the total group discuss:
   a. What was it like to be restricted to the rule of not repeating information?
   b. What did you disclose that you might not have shared otherwise?
   c. How can we use the information we have learned about one another to improve our experience together?

6. Encourage participants to note those people about whom they would like to know more and try to plan time with them during breaks, meals, or after the session.

Variations/ Comments

As each new trio is formed, the facilitator could introduce a new topic, such as:

- What do you do at work?
- What would you advise someone who just started in your profession?
- What is your long-term goal?
- What other kinds of work would you like to do?
- What is your greatest achievement?

Notes to Myself

Self-Sort

Objectives	To identify commonalities among participants
Group Size	Any size
Time Required	Thirty minutes
Physical Setting	Open space for milling about; moveable chairs; small tables
Materials Utilized	Several 3" x 5" Post-It pads (four Post-It sheets per person)

Content and Process

1. Each participant is given four Post-It sheets and is asked to write an important personal characteristic on each. Note that these should be no more than a few words and should be printed in large block letters.

2. The Post-Its are now "pasted" by the participants onto their own clothing.

3. Everyone mills around, reading one another's Post-It labels. Allow five to ten minutes.

4. Ask people to form groups of three or four persons, based on something they think they share with others as determined by what they read on others' Post-It labels.

5. Groups are to meet for five to ten minutes to discuss group members' similarities and differences. Each group is to develop a group name that reflects what they have learned about one another.

6. Each small group briefly reports to the total group its group name, explaining what it is that the small group members originally thought they shared—that is, why they formed—and what they finally concluded they really did share.

Notes to Myself

Team Symbol

Objectives

To develop a sense of teamwork and community

To have participants reveal their uniqueness

To establish a pattern for group decision making

Group Size

Any number because small teams will be formed

Time Required

One hour

Physical Setting

Tables for drawing space and chairs

Materials Utilized

Large pieces of newsprint; 8-1/2" x 11" paper; pencils; colored markers or crayons; tape

Content and Process

1. Ask each person to think of one symbol that represents who they are — perhaps something they value highly, an achievement, special interest, hobby, or possession. Distribute one 8-1/2" x 11" sheet of paper and a pencil to each person. Each person privately is to sketch his/her symbol on paper.

2. Now create groups of four to six people. Each person shares his/her drawing and explains the symbol to the group.

3. Each small group is to develop one large team symbol, incorporating all of the group members' symbols into the new one. They will have to think about what the individuals have in common or think of a theme that applies to everyone.

4. After the team symbols are completed and everyone has "signed" their creations, the total group reconvenes. One team at a time stands, shows, and explains its team symbol. Post each group symbol on the wall.

5. Back in their small groups, ask them to discuss the following questions:

   a. Who took or was assigned leadership?

   b. How accurately was each member's symbol represented?

   c. How did the group decide on its team symbol?

   d. What could your group have done differently to accomplish the task more effectively?

   e. How did individuals' feelings about the group change from when the task was begun to now?

   Notes to Myself

The Builders

Objectives	To develop a sense of teamwork
	To establish a pattern for group decision making
Group Size	Any size because teams of four to six people will be formed
Time Required	Thirty to sixty minutes
Physical Setting	Open floor space
Materials Utilized	Old newspapers; several rolls of masking tape; one brick per group

Content and Process

1. Divide the total group into smaller ones of four to six people and assign them a place to work in the room that will assure some privacy.

2. Give each group a lot of newspaper, tape, and one brick.

3. Explain that when individuals come to a new learning situation, they bring individual characteristics that can enhance the workshop experience. However, now that they are here, they will need to develop patterns of cooperation and teamwork that will positively affect the remaining time together.

4. Give them their task: they are to use newspapers and tape to plan and then build a bridge that is strong enough to hold one brick.

5. As they work, observe how the groups are working together, taking notes on any evidence of leadership and group decision making.

6. When all groups are finished, allow time for comparison of bridges. Ask each group to discuss the following:

    a. Was there a defined leader? If so, how did the group decide who the leader would be?

    b. How did the group determine how to accomplish the task? What did team members do to plan and organize the task?

    c. To what degree were individual ideas incorporated?

    d. What behaviors, attitudes, and communication techniques helped and which ones hindered the process?

7. With the total group, review the small groups' responses to the questions above. Relate what they have learned to the process and content of your workshop.

Variations/ Comments

- You could use other building materials such as tinker toys, building blocks, or Legos. Specify the structure you want built, such as the tallest structure or largest flying machine.

- Increase the challenge with the requirement that the groups have ten minutes to plan the structure, without touching the materials. When ten minutes are up, have the groups simultaneously build their structures, but limit the construction time. Note the times and give prizes to the team that finishes first.

- Or make these last variations even more challenging by having each group select a leader who gives the directions while the other members work holding one hand behind their back.

The Trust Walk

Objectives To develop trust between participants that will enhance their experience together

To help participants experience the meaning of leader vs. follower plus the value of nonverbal communication

Group Size Any size, although it is easier with fewer than fifty people

Time Required Thirty to sixty minutes

Physical Setting Any setting

Materials Utilized One blindfold per dyad

Content and Process

1. Explain the value of increasing trust among group members and how it will enhance their time together. (Tie in your workshop topic, especially if it involves leadership or communication.)

2. Divide the total group into two groups. Have one group stand. Those seated are to close their eyes. Those standing silently mill about, then select a seated partner, and while standing behind the partner's chair, tie a blindfold on him/her.

3. Explain that the "sighted" partners will guide their blindfolded partners on a five-minute walk, but with no verbal directions. The guides are to utilize the existing environment of rooms, hallways, stairs, and outdoors, always considering their partners' safety and willingness to try new experiences.

4. Time the walks for five minutes, giving a one-minute warning.

5. Upon returning, have each blindfolded person remove the blindfold and discover who led him/her. Give them a chance to compare their experiences using these questions:

For Blindfolded Partners:

a. Did you have any idea as to whom your leader might be?

b. What did your leader do that made your walk easy? Difficult?

c. How do you feel toward your partner now?

For Sighted Partners:

a. What made this task difficult for you?

b. How did you plan your walk?

c. How do you feel toward your partner now?

6. With the total group, compare notes on the experience.

7. Reverse the roles, but make sure that the "blind" partner is led by someone new. Suggest that this second round gives the new leaders a chance to apply what they learned while being led.

8. After the five-minute walk, have partners discuss the questions above.

9. Lead a summary discussion with the total group, reviewing the experience and tying it into the content of your workshop and the process you plan to use. Examples are:

a. How can the trust walks enhance our remaining time together?

b. How can you improve the way in which you will communicate?

c. What did this teach us about the role of followers vs. leaders?

The Tie-Up

Objectives   To develop trust between participants that will enhance their experiences together

To give participants an opportunity to get in touch with how it feels to be "tied into" experiences, relationships, and even workshops in which they do not want to be involved

Group Size   Any size

Time Required   As short as thirty minutes or as long as three hours

Physical Setting   Any setting

Materials Utilized   Soft rope or ribbons for tying wrists together

Content and Process

1. Explain that we all find ourselves "tied into" experiences, relationships, and even workshops in which we have no interest. We need to recognize these feelings and determine how to overcome them so we can gain from the situation.

2. Form dyads. Tie the dyads together by their wrists.

3. During the time you have allotted for this activity, give the participants tasks to do, especially some that require writing, walking, and taking breaks.

4. Have dyads discuss their experience using the following questions:

   a. What was your first reaction upon hearing the task?

   b. What problems did you encounter and how did you solve them?

   c. Trace your feelings toward your partner.

   d. What other situations do you face in your personal and work life that you feel "tied into"?

5. Hold a discussion with the total group, summarizing their experiences and what they have learned. Include the following:

   a. How is our motive to work affected when "we do not want to be there"?

   b. How is our learning affected if we do not want to be in a particular workshop or meeting?

   c. How can we reverse this attitude and gain more from the experiences and relationships we are "tied into"?

Variations/ Comments   Have participants record their answers to the questions in Step 4 before discussing them with their group.

Notes to Myself

Sinking Ship

Objectives   To develop a sense of teamwork

To apply a collaborative problem-solving process

Group Size   Up to fifty people; small groups of eight to ten will be formed

Time Required   Sixty minutes

Physical Setting   See Step 1 under "Content and Process"

Materials Utilized   If inside, one chair and masking tape

Content and Process

1. If possible, do this activity outdoors. Locate a rock, log, or stump that you think would hold only about one-half of the number of people you will have in each small group. If you do this indoors, place a chair in an open space and tape a boundary around it, again one-half the space needed to hold everyone from a small group.

2. Divide the total group into smaller groups of eight to ten.

3. Explain that the space you have marked off is their lifeboat. "You have discovered that your ship is sinking and that your group has ten minutes to plan how to save everyone. Everyone must get into the lifeboat. Your group cannot practice on the rock (or chair), but must plan from a distance. Once in the lifeboat, you will have to hold that position for thirty seconds."

4. As the groups plan, observe their planning process. Call time after ten minutes.

5. Have the small groups draw straws to determine the order in which the groups will implement their plans. Have each group execute its plans for getting into the "lifeboats" while the other groups observe.

6. Have the groups discuss the following questions:
   a. Did leaders emerge or were they selected?
   b. How well were everyone's ideas used?
   c. What caused your group to succeed, or to fail?
   d. What could you have done differently?
   e. How can we use what we have learned to enhance our learning and remaining time together?

Variations/ Comments Do a second round using a different obstacle, more difficult conditions (like only one hand), or with new group members. Encourage the participants to apply what they have learned.

Notes to Myself

The Machine

Objectives	To develop a sense of teamwork
	To help the participants comprehend a difficult concept
Group Size	Ten to twenty people
Time Required	Thirty minutes
Physical Setting	Open space
Materials Utilized	None
Content and Process	1. Explain that a fully functioning group is like a well-oiled machine. Each part is important, but the interrelationships between parts is most important. Indicate that we are going to create a "Human Machine."
	2. Ask one person to come into the open space and act out, repeatedly, one motion with an accompanying sound.
	3. Ask the remaining participants to spontaneously "hook into" the machine, adding a complimentary repetitive motion and sound. Guide the creation by making sure each person has hooked into the machine before the next person is added.
	4. When the machine is functioning fully, ask one "part" to malfunction. Observe what happens.

5. Resume seats and discuss the experience using the following questions:

   a. How did you decide what "part" you would be?

   b. What happened when one part malfunctioned?

   c. How does the functioning of our "Human Machine" relate to our experiences in working with others?

   d. How can we apply what we have learned to our group effort here?

Variations/ Comments

Select a concept you plan to develop during your workshop, such as competition, communication, work, play, lazy, team. Develop a machine that is a "Communication Machine," or a "Work Machine," etc.

Notes to Myself

Patterns

Objectives   To examine how people "naturally" form into small groups

To focus on communication structures and processes

Group Size   Between fifteen and fifty people

Time Required   Thirty to sixty minutes

Physical Setting   Tables and chairs

Materials Utilized   Pens, pencils, paper; newsprint; markers; masking tape

Content and Process

1. Post a sign indicating that participants are to enter the meeting room and make themselves comfortable, awaiting the facilitator who may be delayed a few minutes. The facilitator and any staff keep out of the meeting room and out of sight for ten to fifteen minutes after the formal starting time for the session.

2. After ten to fifteen minutes, the facilitator enters the meeting room and asks everyone to take out pencil and paper (or pass out paper and a pencil to each person).

3. The facilitator instructs the participants to "draw a picture" of the conversations that occurred during the previous ten minutes. Each participant should be symbolized by a circle, with lines and arrows drawn to show who talked to whom. Allow about five minutes for this.

4. Form small groups of three or four, mixing people from different parts of the room. Each group is to inspect the diagrams produced by its members and develop a single "correct" diagram. The group diagram is to be drawn on a large sheet of newsprint, using a marker so that it can be seen easily. When the groups finish their diagrams, they are to post them on the wall, using masking tape. Allow about ten minutes.

5. Next, have each group briefly explain its diagram to the entire group. The facilitator directs the participants' attention to similarities and differences among the various diagrams. Some points that can be made include:

   a. The fact that there are some definite common patterns that are found on all or almost all of the diagrams. Why is this the case?

   b. The fact that there are some patterns that are unique to just one (or perhaps shared by just two) of the small groups. Why is this the case?

   c. What was it that made some patterns clearly noticeable by many participants while others (that may have actually existed) were only noticed by a few people?

   d. What would have happened to the patterns if more time had been allowed, if the facilitator had entered the room after another ten, twenty, or thirty minutes? Would some or all of the patterns we saw have been stable?

   e. What was the basis for the patterns we saw? Why did a particular pattern arise? Will such observable patterns of communication arise in any group of strangers?

7. Tie this experience into the objectives of your workshop: how their "natural" groupings can both help and hinder the workshop experience.

5

Dipping into the Content

Often you have only a short period of time to implement your design. The activities in this chapter can help move your participants quickly into the content of your program while you are getting them warmed-up.

Also these activities can be used for your workshops that run several days. Use a different one to introduce each new component of your design or at the beginning of each day.

Additional activities that also fit this chapter's purposes but are found elsewhere in this book are:

The Pre-Test

Objectives To identify participants' knowledge of or attitudes toward the workshop topics

Group Size Any size

Time Required Depends on the length of the pre-test

Physical Setting Nothing required

Materials Utilized Prepared pre-test

Content and Process

1. Determine the purpose of pre-testing your participants. For example, if you need the information so you can plan your workshop around their needs, prepare and administer the pre-test well in advance of the program. If you want to validate your workshop design and are willing or able to adapt the design on the spot, then you could administer the pre-test at the beginning of the program. Prepare your questions carefully.

2. Most people become anxious when tested so explain the purpose of your pre-test. Your desire to get the participants interested in your topics may backfire if they feel "put on the spot."

3. Determine how you will tabulate the results. If you administer the pre-test on-site, you could:
   a. do a hand poll of the answers, or
   b. collect them and have a second individual score them while you continue with the workshop.

4. Depending on your purpose, schedule a post-test either at the end of your program or mail it to them one month later.

**Variations/
Comments**

- Keep the atmosphere light by offering humorous prizes or special rewards, such as being first in line for lunch.

- After individuals have tried their best to answer the questions, have them form small groups and work together on the answers. Keep the tests that are completed individually separate from those done in a group so they can see the value of group vs. individual efforts.

Notes to Myself

I Know. . . I Don't Know. . .

Objectives To identify what the participants want to know about the topic of the workshop so that the experience will be relevant

To identify resources within the group that will help to meet specific needs of the participants

Group Size Up to thirty people

Time Required Thirty to sixty minutes

Physical Setting Round tables for up to eight people; blank wall

Materials Utilized Newsprint; markers; masking tape

Content and Process

1. Introduce the idea that each of us comes to a workshop with prior knowledge of the planned topics and also with specific questions and needs. Emphasize that you, as a facilitator, are only one resource person present; that collectively, group members probably have answers to any question that may be raised during the workshop.

2. If your group has more than fifteen people, do the following activity first in small groups at their tables and then discuss with the total group.
   a. State the workshop topic (leadership, supervision, conflict, etc.).
   b. Ask them to list on a piece of newsprint everything they know about the topic.

c. Next, have them make a second list of other things they would like to know about the topic, or have questions or concerns about.

d. After the lists are completed, post them on the wall.

3. Next, match up resources with stated needs and concerns. For example, if one person says he/she is having trouble supervising young employees because their values are so different, determine if any other group member has had some success in that area. You could immediately tap that resource person's knowledge, or call on his/her help when you get to that part of your workshop. If you had not intended to discuss that topic, suggest that the two people meet during a break or over lunch.

4. Keep the newsprint lists posted. As questions are answered, check them off the lists. Before participants leave, make sure everyone who raised a question or concern is given some resource if possible.

Notes to Myself

Best/Worst

Objectives	To help participants identify specific characteristics or problems they have had with the workshop topic
Group Size	Up to fifty people; the group is divided into smaller groups of four to six
Time Required	Fifteen to thirty minutes
Physical Setting	Tables and chairs for small groups
Materials Utilized	Newsprint; markers; tape
Content and Process	

1. Based on your proposed workshop topics, select a pair of antonyms such as:

   Best/Worst — Boss, Leader, Parent, Employee, Customer. . .

   Easiest/Hardest — Task, Problem, Job, Role. . .

   Biggest/Smallest — Problem, Dilemma, Risk, Conflict. . .

2. Form small groups of four to six people.

3. Give each group two sheets of newsprint and markers. Ask them to label the top of each sheet with one of the antonyms you introduce.

4. Each small group brainstorms a list of everything that comes to mind when they think of each antonym. For example, if your antonyms are "Best Boss" and "Worst Boss," they would list characteristics of the best and worst kinds of bosses they have experienced. Make sure that they include all answers that come to mind, whether or not they seem ridiculous.

5. After about fifteen minutes, have the small groups post their lists and highlight some parts (or all) of their lists.

6. Relate what they have recorded to your workshop objectives and topics.

Notes to Myself

The Computer

Objectives   To help participants focus on the topic of the workshop

Group Size   Groups of eight people

Time Required   Ten to fifteen minutes

Physical Setting   Open space or round tables

Materials Utilized   None

Content and Process

1. Form circles of eight people, either standing or sitting.

2. Explain that each person comes to the workshop with certain knowledge and attitudes. Each person will be asked to contribute one piece of information into a "Human Computer" so that together the workshop topic or concept will be more clear.

3. The leader "enters" a sentence stem based on the topic of the workshop into an imaginary computer. Examples might be:

    a. Integration is. . .

    b. Supervisors. . .

    c. New employees. . .

    d. Conflict means. . .

    e. Men are. . .

    f. Women are. . .

4. After the key words are "entered," each person in turn adds one word or appropriate punctuation mark. Continue until each person has made at least one contribution and the sentence is completed.

5. Do additional rounds until you think the participants have sufficiently clarified the workshop topic, helping you to move into the content of your program.

6. Tie the sentences the groups developed into your program objectives and topics.

Notes to Myself

Four Corners

Objectives To have participants quickly identify with a role or preference or take a position on a particular topic or issue

Group Size This works well with large numbers of people

Time Required Fifteen to thirty minutes, depending on how many groups of words you want to use

Physical Setting Open space with four defined corners

Materials Utilized Newsprint; markers; tape

Content and Process

1. Explain that each of us has established views or identifies with certain positions on a topic.

2. Explain that you will be presenting a group of four words (or four statements), each of which will be posted in one of the corners of the room. As each set is posted, participants should move to the corner that has the word they identify with (or the statement that best fits their position on that issue).

3. Select your groups of words from the samples that follow or create your own.

4. After the first set of words is read and posted and participants have moved to their chosen corner, have those in the same corner discuss why they made that choice.

5. Then, lead a short discussion with the total group:

    a. Why did you select that corner?

    b. What would you like to ask those in any other corner?

6. Repeat the process using a new group of words.

7. The number of rounds you do will depend on the group's energy, plus the number of concepts, values, or roles you want participants to clarify.

Sample Word Groups

Professional	Intellectual	Compromiser
Administrator	Emotional	Collaborator
Teacher	Physical	Competitor
Counselor	Spiritual	Confonter
Doer	Work	Women
Leader	Sex	Men
Follower	Family	Children
Member	Self	Men and Women
Cool	Uniter	
Hot	Co-opter	
Cold	Fighter	
Warm	Flighter	

Variations/ Comments

Have the participants take a stand on a particular issue or topic related to the workshop. This could be done by posting statements that represent four different viewpoints on the same issue. Or, post four different issues relating to a single topic. In either case, the participants select the viewpoint or issue with which they most closely identify.

My Experience As. . .

Objectives   To identify participants' experience with the topic of the workshop

To have participants get better acquainted

Group Size   Any size; small groups of six to eight people will be formed

Time Required   Thirty minutes

Physical Setting   Tables and chairs

Materials Utilized   Handout; pencils/pens; flipchart, chalkboard, or overhead projector; markers

Content and Process

1. Develop a handout similar to the example provided with this exercise that is based on your workshop topic.

2. Explain that we each have a wealth of experience that can help us dip into the workshop topic on _____.

3. Form small groups of six to eight participants. Pass the handouts and ask them to complete Part I.

4. In small groups, participants share the experience they have selected.

5. Each person completes Part II.

6. Participants are asked to introduce themselves to the total group by sharing one answer from Questions 1-5 of Part II.

7. Use their responses to Question 6 to develop a list of their objectives for the workshop. Post these so they can be referred to and checked off as the workshop progresses.

Example

My Experience as a Negotiator

Part I   *Directions:* Negotiating is something we do every day of our lives. Perhaps we do not think of it as negotiating. But every time we try to gain the favor of people from whom we want something, we are *negotiating*. Below is a list of typical negotiation situations. Select or invent one that really tested your skill. How did you negotiate your way into or out of it?

An appliance salesperson
A surgeon for his/her fee
A policeman prepared to write you a traffic ticket
Your son for the use of the family car
A hotel clerk who has just told you there are no rooms
    despite your guaranteed reservation
Your boss for a raise
Your landlord for a decorating allowance
Your teenage daughter for the time she must be home
    from a date
Your supervisor for a challenging assignment
A car dealer for the purchase of a new car
A restaurant cashier reluctant to accept your personal check
Your family or friends for a particular vacation
A claims adjuster for a more fair settlement
A seller for a lower price on his/her home
Your spouse or friend for. . .
A department store clerk for a credit
A maitre d' for a better table
A particular movie with your friends
(your choice)

Part II   *Directions:* You will use this part of the exercise to introduce yourself to the entire group. Thinking back over your professional experiences as a negotiator, make a few brief notes in response to the following statements.

1. To me, effective negotiation is. . .
2. I learned to negotiate by. . .
3. My greatest success as a negotiator came when. . .
4. My worst failure as a negotiator came when. . .
5. My greatest fear as a negotiator is. . .
6. What I would like to do better as a negotiator is. . .

The Continuum

Objectives To show that there are many positions on any issue or role

Group Size Up to thirty people

Time Required Fifteen to thirty minutes

Physical Setting For the variation, open space to create one long line of participants

Materials Utilized Newsprint or chalkboard to draw continuum

Content and Process

1. Explain that with any group of people and with any topic or issue there will be a range of opinions.

2. Draw a long line on the newsprint or chalkboard and label it with your workshop topic or issue. Then identify the two extreme positions. See the examples with this exercise.

3. After you have explained the positions on the continuum, ask individuals to identify where they are on the continuum. Put their initials at the position they identify.

4. Another question you could ask is, "Where would you like to be on this continuum?"

Sample Continuums

In a workshop on "Risk Taking," the continuum might look like this:

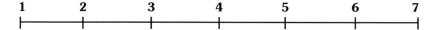

| Rarely Takes Risk | Considered Risk Taker | Extreme Risk Taker |

For a leadership workshop, the continuum might have several points on the continuum labeled:

1   2   3   4   5   6   7

1 = I have never been a leader and never will be

2 = Once in awhile I emerge as a leader

3 = I lead only those whom I know well

4 = I do some leading and some following

5 = I am a leader in many groups, depending on who is in the group and the task at hand

6 = I am almost always the leader

7 = I have always been and always will be the leader

Variations/ Comments

Indicate an imaginary line down the center of the room. As you did on paper or the chalkboard, label the extreme positions. Have participants stand and form one line based on their positions. They will need to discuss their views in order to determine their positions.

Notes to Myself

Getting to Know You

Objectives   To help the participants get into the program content while they are getting acquainted

Group Size   Any size

Time Required   Fifteen to thirty minutes

Physical Setting   Open space for milling about; chairs for trios

Materials Utilized   Prepare a handout with questions relevant to the program content. Include directions and a space for note taking. You might also supply pencils or pens.

Content and Process

1. As the participants arrive, have them mill about meeting others until they find two other people with whom they would like to form a trio.

2. Have the trios move to the chairs and provide each person with a copy of the handout.

3. Have the trios discuss the questions on the handout for about ten minutes.

4. Now hold a discussion with the total group. Relate the questions and their responses to your agenda and topic.

**Variations/
Comments**

- Instead of forming trios immediately, ask everyone to mill about, talking with as many different people as they can within the time limit, discussing the questions and making notes. Individuals may want to focus on one question and poll everyone they talk with; others may choose to ask others a variety of questions.

- Form a series of trios. Your first trio could be composed of males and females; your second composed of the same gender; your third could be a merging of a trio of men plus a trio of women. Or, form trios of people with the same or similar characteristics that might be related to the workshop content. For example: job; married/single/children/no children; single child/one of several children; place of birth; hobby; etc.

Notes to Myself

6

Re-grouping Participants

Often activities are needed to help re-group participants while they are getting better acquainted or because you would like them to work with different people to expand their personal network. The activities in this section can be fun and energizing.

For longer programs, plan to use several of these activities to add some variety to your program design.

An additional activity that fits the purposes of this chapter but is found elsewhere in this book is:

Colors or Numbers

Objectives	To re-group participants as they register
Group Size	Any size
Time Required	Ten minutes
Physical Setting	Table for registration
Materials Utilized	Gummed name tags or table tents; optional colored, gummed dots
Content and Process	1. Determine, in advance, the number of groups you will need during the first part of your program. For example, if you need eight groups, you could number your name tags or table tents in sequential order from 1-8, preparing as many tags or tents with each table number as is required by the total group size. Or, if you need fewer groups, you could code the tags or tents with different colored, gummed dots for each group.
	2. As participants register, give them their name tags or table tents.
	3. Once the workshop has started, and you now need small groups, re-group them using either your pre-assigned colors or numbers as they appear on the tags/tents.
	4. Later, if you need a new grouping arrangement, re-group with complimentary colors, or odd numbers with even numbers.

Variations/ Comments Use gummed seals with different symbols such as animals, flowers, zodiac signs, etc. In addition, you could allow the participants to select their tag or card with the symbol they prefer (prepare the required number of tags/tents in advance).

Notes to Myself

The Diversity Mix

Objectives To form small groups from the total group based on the greatest degree of diversity possible

Group Size Any size

Time Required Fifteen to thirty minutes

Physical Setting Large open space for milling about; round tables and chairs for groups of up to eight

Materials Utilized In advance of the session, write the categories and points on a flipchart, chalkboard, or transparency.

Content and Process

1. Explain that every group of people contains a diversity of backgrounds, interests, skills, roles, and values. Usually, society rewards us for conforming and diminishes the value of diversity. In this activity, diversity will be rewarded. We will be forming new groups based on as much diversity as possible.

2. Select approximately five categories from those provided with this exercise.

3. Present the categories and explain how points are assigned—basically, each person gets one point for every characteristic he/she possesses. However, when group scores are tallied, if more than one person in the group has the same characteristic, it can only be counted as one point for the group. For example, for the characteristic of gender, if there are five men and

one woman in a group, the woman gets one point and only one point is allotted for all five men. For ethnicity, each different ethnic part of one's heritage counts one point, so a person with Scotch, English, and German might contribute three points to his/her group. But Scotch, for example, would only be counted once if a second person or other people are also Scotch.

4. After the participants are clear on their individual points, have them stand and mingle, "hawking" their worth (obviously, if you are the only one of a particular category in a group, you will be valuable). The participants' goal is to form small groups that are as diversified as possible and therefore will have the most points. (Determine the group size by dividing the total number of participants by six to eight. The groups need to be equal in size or you will have to do extra math later to balance out the points.)

5. When the small groups are formed and seated at a table, have one person record the group's points for each category. Be prepared to help them determine the points for which they qualify.

6. Build up the ending dramatically as you ask the groups for their scores. Give the most diverse group a reward, such as the privilege of being first in line for coffee or lunch.

7. Discuss the experience in the total group with questions such as:

   a. What category helped your group obtain the most points?

   b. What was a unique fact you discovered about one person or your group as a whole?

   c. How can you take what you have learned about each other and make this workshop experience more rewarding?

Examples of Categories	Categories	Points
	Gender	1 Point
	Race	1 Point
	Ethnicity	1 Point per ethnic heritage; individuals with several different ethnic parts in their backgrounds have the advantage.
	Age	1 Point for each decade represented: under 20, 21-29, 30-39, 40-49, 50-59, over 60.
	Organizational Roles	1 Point for each different job description
	Type of Organization	1 Point for each different type of organization such as banks, manufacturing, education, church, associations
	Origins	1 Point per state or country (either where born or living currently)
	Experience (as manager, teacher. . .)	Points for number of years: 1 point for under 2 years; 2 points for 2-10 years; 3 points for over 10 years.
	Familiarity	1 Point for each person unknown to you

Notes to Myself

Meet and Match

Objectives   To form several small groups from the total group

To facilitate conversation between people in a climate of fun

Group Size   Minimum of forty people; form groups of eight to ten

Time Required   Thirty to sixty minutes

Physical Setting   Open space for milling about; round tables and chairs for groups of eight to ten

Materials Utilized   Handouts

Content and Process

1. Prepare an instruction sheet. Select the number of categories needed based on the number of participants (one category per group of eight to ten). Prepare the individual slips of category items. (Use the categories provided with this exercise or create others that apply to your workshop topic.)

2. As participants arrive, give them a copy of the instruction sheet. Ask them to mill about until they find the other members of their group (seven to nine people, depending on the group size selected).

3. When they have their groups together (or at the designated time), ask them to select a table.

4. At this point, you might serve a meal. However, you could use this activity just as a means of forming smaller groups.

5. Questions that could be discussed within the small groups include:

   a. How did you feel as you were asked to find others in your category?

   b. What made it difficult or easy to accomplish this task?

   c. What else do the team members have in common?

   d. What brought you to this workshop?

Sample Instruction Sheet

Each of you have received a slip of paper on which is written an item that fits into a particular category. In the total group, there are seven (or appropriate number) other people whose items fit your same category. Your goal is to find those other people and form a group. You will then be asked to sit at one of the tables.

Clue: Your item will fit into one of these categories.

Sports	Authors
Card Games	Musical Instruments
Television Shows	Food
Automobiles	Types of Music
Presidents	Plants

Examples within Categories
To Use for Individual Slips of Paper

Sports	Baseball, Football, Tennis, Golf, Racketball, Volleyball, Soccer, Ping Pong
Card Games	Poker, Canasta, Bridge, Fish, Old Maid
Television Shows	*Hill Street Blues*, *Newhart*, *Cheers*, *Moonlighting*, *thirtysomething*, *Six O'Clock News*, *Today Show*, *Tonight Show*, *Masterpiece Theatre*
Automobiles	Camaro, Corvette, Toyota, Manza, VW, Fiat
Presidents	Washington, Lincoln, Roosevelt, Ford, Kennedy, Carter, Reagan, Grant
Universities	Washington, Duke, Harvard, Princeton, Cornell, Texas, Berkeley, Radcliffe
Authors	Stone, Porter, Friedan, Toffler, Jaffee, Michener
Musical Instruments	Piano, Violin, Trumpet, Harp, Guitar, Banjo, Trombone, Drums
Foods	Pizza, Cake, Stew, Spaghetti, Soup, Salad, Rolls, Milk
Types of Music	Bluegrass, Classical, Blues, Jazz, Rock, Country, Opera, Swing
Plants	Fern, Violet, Geranium, Poinsettia, Gardenia, Rose, Spider Plant, Daisy

Mix and Mingle

Objectives   To help participants become acquainted with each other before they form smaller groups

To provide an opportunity for participants to identify their own personal and professional expectations for the workshop

Group Size   Any size

Time Required   Ten minutes

Physical Setting   Open space for milling about

Materials Utilized   A hand-mike for groups over twenty-five; chairs; newsprint, chalkboard, or overhead projector; markers

Content and Process

Part I: Getting Acquainted

1. Explain that we often come to a workshop or conference without knowing others, sometimes leaving still knowing very few people. Ask everyone to stand and move into the open area. Explain that you will be giving them several sets of instructions.

2. First, ask them to scan the other participants with their eyes. Do this silently.

3. Now, ask them to move slowly but silently around the room. After thirty seconds, tell them to walk quickly but silently.

4. Then, ask them to smile brightly at each person they pass while walking slowly.

5. Now, ask them to make a serious facial expression as they walk around.

6. Next, ask them to shake hands silently with others.

7. Now, they are to place both hands on the shoulders of other people, adding verbal greetings as they mill about like "Hello," or "Hi Brother" or "Hi Sister."

8. Last, have them select one partner from all the people they have seen. Each pair should combine with two or three more pairs to form a discussion group of six to eight people. Participants should then relocate their personal items and chairs with their new group.

Part II: Clarifying Expectations

1. Explain that people usually have certain expectations of a workshop or conference. There is a value in making these expectations clear if people are to gain the most from the program.

2. In their small groups, ask each person to share one professional reason why they are attending this workshop. Allow two minutes per person.

3. Next, ask each person to share a personal reason for coming (two minutes each).

4. Lead a total group review of expectations, asking for volunteers to give a summary of expectations, goals, concerns, and issues that emerged during the small group discussions. Tabulate key points on newsprint, chalkboard, or overhead transparency. Relate what is said to the workshop or conference goals and activities.

Variations/ Comments   Either Part I or Part II could be used alone.

Notes to Myself

Team Signal

Objectives	To form small groups out of the total group
	To provide a playful way for participants to develop a sense of unity and teamwork
Group Size	Any size
Time Required	Fifteen minutes
Physical Setting	Open space for milling about
Materials Utilized	None

Content and Process

1. Without others' knowledge, each person is given the name of an animal. (You might have a coded number on the back of table tents or pass out cards.)

2. Everyone puts on a blindfold and stands in the open area.

3. As they carefully mill about, each person is to mimic the sound of their animal and locate the other "animals" like them in the group.

4. When all the "animals" of the same kind find each other, take off the blindfolds and let them discuss the experience before you introduce a new task.

Variations/ Comments

- Form small groups. Let each plan a signal for their own group. Mix everyone up, blindfold them, and have the small groups find each other. Give a prize to the group that does it the quickest.

- Signals could also be nonverbal, such as two hands on shoulders or special handshakes. This could be more threatening to people who dislike touching others.

Notes to Myself

I'm OK — You're OK

Objectives   To form small groups out of the total group

To provide an atmosphere where positive affirmation is accepted and encouraged

Group Size   Any size

Time Required   Fifteen minutes

Physical Setting   Open space for milling about

Materials Utilized   None

Content and Process

1. Explain the value of giving and receiving positive affirmations, both for the workshop time together and in other settings.

2. Ask everyone to stand in the open space. As they mill about, each person is to say, "Hi, there. I'm wonderful and my name is. . ."

3. After a minute, change the sentence stem to: "Hi. I know you're wonderful. What's your name?"

4. After a minute, change the sentence stem to: "Hi. I'm great because. . ."

5. After a minute, change the sentence stem to: "I'd like you in my group because. . ."

6. After one minute, instruct the participants to form small groups of four to six. (The exact number depends on the size of the groups you will need for the next part of your program.)

7. Allow time for reactions to this experience and to tie it into the objectives of your workshop.

Notes to Myself

The Five-Course Meal

Objectives

To form several small groups out of the total group

Group Size

Any size

Time Required

Sixty minutes or more—whatever time it takes for one meal

Physical Setting

Round tables with chairs for up to six people

Materials Utilized

None

Content and Process

1. Well before the meal, at the location where this will be done, explain your purpose and procedure with those involved in serving the meal so that you do not make it unusually hard on them.

2. Before entering the dining room, ask participants to select any table, but not to sit with people they know well or just worked with in the prior segment of the program.

3. Serve a beverage and ask the participants to exchange names, roles, and other pleasantries.

4. Ask two people from each table to go to a new table, taking any utensils or glasses they may have used. Now, introduce a new topic for them to discuss at this table. Each of the topics to be introduced could relate to your workshop and/or to areas in which you want participants to know each other better. Serve the soup course.

5. Ask two new people to move to a new table, again taking used table settings along. Introduce a new topic for discussion and serve the salad and bread course.

6. Ask two new people to move, introduce a new topic, and serve the main course.

7. Ask two new people to move, serve coffee and dessert, and introduce the final topic.

Variations/ Comments It may be easier for those preparing and serving the meal to set up the courses buffet style, although this would add considerably more time and confusion.

Notes to Myself

Potpourri

Objectives	To re-group participants quickly
Group Size	Any size
Time Required	Ten minutes
Physical Setting	Any setting
Materials Utilized	None
Content and Process	When you need to re-group participants quickly, select one of the following ways.

1. *By Role:* First, group all teachers vs. administrators; or leadpersons vs. forepersons; or supervisors vs. managers, etc. Then, mix them up by roles.

2. *By Gender:* First, group men vs. women; then, mixed genders.

3. *By Age:* First, group by same decade; then, mixed ages.

4. *By Counting Off*

5. *By Shoe Size*

6. *By Hair or Eye Color*

7. *By Food Preferences:* meat vs. vegetarian; dessert vs. salad

8. *By Energy:* morning, afternoon, or evening people

9. *By Geographical Preference:* seashore, mountain, city, or plains

10. *By Color Preferences*

11. *By Sports Preferences*

12. *By Favorite Types of Music:* classical, bluegrass, rock, or country

13. *By Favorite Meal:* breakfast, lunch, dinner, or midnight snack

14. *By Home States*

15. *By Shared Views:* Group all those who agree on a given topic or issue; then mix them up again.

Notes to Myself

People to People

Objectives
A high-energy, fun activity involving physical movement and group mixing. Use as an energizer—ideal for after lunch or prior to the evening session. Best used when group members are relatively comfortable with each other.

Group Size
Any size

Time Required
Ten to fifteen minutes

Physical Setting
Large open space

Materials Utilized
None

Content and Process

1. Have the participants gather in the open space and pick a partner. If the group is an odd number, have one person step aside for the demonstration round—then he/she can conduct the next few commands. If the group has an even number, the facilitator will call all of the commands.

2. Explain that the exercise is to be nonverbal.

3. Different phrases will be called out. They are to follow the command with their partner. When they hear the phrase "People to People" called out, they are to pair up immediately with a different partner—they cannot have the same partner twice.

4. Each time there is a new pairing, someone is left without a partner if the number is odd. That person can call the next few commands, then go for a partner after he/she calls out, "People to People."

5. Partners have to hold each pose until the next command is called out.

6. Sample calls: elbows to elbows; knees to knees; right hand to right hand; etc. Calls can be cumulative such as: back to back — pause — lock arms.

7. It becomes harder to find a new partner. Stop the process when most of the possible pairings have been experienced.

Notes to Myself

All My Friends

Objectives	To raise group energy before a work session
Group Size	Up to twenty people
Time Required	Ten to fifteen minutes
Physical Setting	Large open space
Materials Utilized	Sturdy chairs — one per participant
Content and Process	

1. Ask the participants to form a circle with their chairs. The facilitator stands in the middle.

2. The purpose of the game is to get out of the center. To do this, you get more than one person to move and attempt to occupy one of their chairs while they are moving.

3. The facilitator explains that everyone who fits the description called out by the person in the center must get up and occupy a different seat. The person in the center then tries to capture one of those chairs. Whoever is left over goes to the center.

4. Examples of descriptions are: "all my friends have blue eyes"; "all my friends are left-handed"; "all my friends wear sports shoes." Statements such as, "all my friends like money (or sex)" usually gets the whole group moving.

5. Stop when about half the group has been "caught."

6. This exercise can get rough. Invite people with physical concerns to opt out.

Notes to Myself

Acknowledgments

I would like to give credit to the following people for their contributions to this collection of exercises. My special thanks go to Rollin Glaser, Christine Glaser, Marshall Sashkin, and John Jones for their efforts in preparing this Second Edition.

Chapter Two

The Whip

"The Whip" is often used by Dr. Sidney Simon. For additional uses of the "Values Whip," see *Values Clarification: A Handbook of Practical Strategies for Teachers and Students* by Sidney Simon, Leland Howe, and Howard Kirschenbaum (New York, NY: Hart Publishing, 1972) p. 130.

Issues and Obstacles

Delores Leone

Chapter Three

The Name Tag

I first learned this name tag activity from Dr. Sidney Simon and since then have seen other trainers use it with various categories.

My Personal Shield

Rollin Glaser

What's in a Name?

The last variation is more completely described in *Playfair* by Matt Weinstein and Joel Goodman (San Luis Obispo, CA: Impact Publishers, 1980) pp. 65-66.

Name Your Uniqueness

Another version of "Naming Your Uniqueness" is described as, ". . .Ing Name Tags" in *Values Clarification.* . . pp. 174-176.

Are You More. . .

Adapted from *Values Clarification.* . . p. 94.

The Real Me

Rollin Glaser

You Can't Tell a Book by Its Cover

Rev. Margaret Rush

Feelings Wheel

Gerry Weinstein invented the original "Here-and-Now Wheel" from which adaptations have been made. For a more complete description of the "Feelings Wheel" see *Playfair*. . . p. 134.

Chapter Four

Self-Sort

Dr. Marshall Sashkin

The Builders

Vandla Julnes

Patterns

Dr. Marshall Sashkin

Chapter Five

The Pre-Test

For additional methods of pre-workshop assessment read "Assessing Needs" in *Planning, Conducting and Evaluating Workshops* by Larry Nolan Davis and Earl McCallon (Austin, TX: Learning Concepts, 1974) p. 35.

My Experience As. . .

Rollin Glaser

The Continuum

The "Values Continuum," a basic strategy of "Values Clarification," is often used by Sidney Simon. For more examples and uses in the classroom *see Values Clarification*. . . p. 116.

Chapter Six

I'm OK—You're OK

Adapted from an activity submitted by Vandla Julnes.

People to People

Dr. John E. Jones

All My Friends

Dr. John E. Jones